THE FICTION FACTORY

The Fiction Factory

Being the Experience of a Writer who, for Twenty-two Years, has kept a Story-mill Grinding Successfully

by William Wallace Cook,
writing as John Milton Edwards

Norton Creek Press

http://www.nortoncreekpress.com

ISBN 978-0-9819284-9-4

Norton Creek Press
36475 Norton Creek Road
Blodgett Oregon 97326
http://www.nortoncreekpress.com

Originally published in 1912 by The Editor.

10 9 8 7 6 5 4 3 2 1

Contents of Chapters.

THE WRITER
TO THE READER

It was in 1893 that John Milton Edwards (who sets his hand to this book of experiences and prefers using the third person to overworking the egotistical pronoun) turned wholly to his pen as a means of livelihood. In this connection, of course, the word "pen" is figurative. What he really turned to was his good friend, the Typewriter.

For two years previous to this (to him) momentous event he had hearkened earnestly to the counsel that "literature is a good stick but a poor crutch," and had cleaved to a position as paymaster for a firm of contractors solely because of the pay envelope that insured food and raiment. Spare hours alone were spent in his Fiction Factory. In the summer of 1893, however, when his evening and Sunday work brought returns that dwarfed his salary as paymaster, he had a heart to heart talk with Mrs. John Milton Edwards, and, as a result, the paymaster-crutch was dropped by the wayside. This came to pass not without many fears and anxieties, and later there arrived gray days when the literary pace became unsteady and John Milton turned wistful eyes backward in the direction of his discarded crutch. But he never returned to pick it up.

From then till now John Milton Edwards has worked early and late in his Factory, and his output has supported himself and wife and enabled him to bear a number of other financial responsibilities. There have been fat years and lean—years when plenty invited

foolish extravagance and years when poverty compelled painful sacrifices—yet John Milton Edwards can
truly say that the work has been its own exceeding great
reward.

With never a "best seller" nor a successful play to
run up his income, John Milton has, in a score and two
years of work, wrested more than $100,000 from the
tills of the publishers. Short stories, novelettes, serials,
books, a few moving picture scenarios and a little verse
have all contributed to the sum total. Industry was
rowelled by necessity, and when a short story must fill
the flour barrel, a poem buy a pair of shoes or a serial
take up a note at the bank, the muse is provided with an
atmosphere at which genius balks. True, Genius has
emerged triumphant from many a Grub street attic, but
that was in another day when conditions were different
from what they are now. In these twentieth century
times the writer must give the public what the publisher
thinks the public wants. Although the element of quality is a *sine qua non,* it seems not to be incompatible
with the element of quantity.

It is hoped that this book will be found of interest
to writers, not alone to those who have arrived but also
to those who are on the way. Writers with name and
fame secure may perhaps be entertained, while writers
who are struggling for recognition may discover something helpful here and there throughout John Milton
Edwards' twenty-two years of literary endeavor. And
is it too fair a hope that the reader of fiction will here
find something to his taste? He has an acquaintance
with the finished article, and it may chance that he has
the curiosity to discover how the raw material was

taken, beaten into shape and finally laid before his eyes in his favorite periodical.

John Milton Edwards, in the pages that follow, will spin the slender thread of a story recounting his successes and failures. Extracts of correspondence between him and his publishers will be introduced, and other personal matters will be conjured with, by way of illustrating the theme and giving the text a helpful value. This slender thread of narrative will be broken at intervals to permit of sandwiching in a few chapters not germane to the story but *en rapport* with the work which made the story possible. In other words, while life goes forward within the Factory-walls it will not be amiss to give some attention to the Factory itself, to its equipment and methods, and to anything of possible interest that has to do with its output.

And finally, of course John Milton Edwards is not the author's real name. Shielded by a *nom de plume,* the author's experiences here chronicled may be of the most intimate nature. In point of fact, they will be helpful and entertaining in a direct ratio with their sincerity and frankness.

"A LITTLE GIFT"

A little gift I have of words,
  A little talent, Lord, is all,
And yet be mine the faith that girds
  An humble heart for duty's call.

Where Genius soars to distant skies,
  And plumes herself in proud acclaim,
O Thou, let plodding talent prize
The modest goal, the lesser fame.

Let this suffice, make this my code,
  As I go forward day by day,
To cheer one heart upon life's road,
  To ease one burden by the way.

I would not scale the mountain-peak,
  But I would have the strength of ten
To labor for the poor and weak,
  And win my way to hearts of men.

A little gift Thou gavest me,
  A little talent, Lord, is all,
Yet humble as my art may be
  I hold it waiting for Thy call.

September 20, 1911.   John Milton Edwards.

THE FICTION FACTORY

I.

AUT FICTION,
AUT NULLUS.

"Well, my dear," said John Milton Edwards, miserably uncertain and turning to appeal to his wife, "which shall it be—to write or not to write?"

"To write," was the answer, promptly and boldly, "to do nothing else but write."

John Milton wanted her to say that, and yet he did not. Her conviction, orally expressed, had all the ring of true metal; yet her husband, reflecting his own inner perplexities, heard a false note suggesting the base alloy of uncertainty.

"Hadn't we better think it over?" he quibbled.

"You've been thinking it over for two years, John, and this month is the first time your returns from your writing have ever been more than your salary at the office. If you can be so successful when you are obliged to work nights and Sundays—and most of the time with your wits befogged by office routine—what could you not do if you spent ALL your time in your Fiction Factory?"

"It may be," ventured John Milton, "that I could do better work, snatching a few precious moments from those everlasting pay-rolls, than by giving all my time and attention to my private Factory."

"Is that logical?" inquired Mrs. John Milton.

"I don't know, my dear, whether it's logical or not. We're dealing with a psychological mystery that has never been broken to harness. Suppose I have the whole day before me and sit down at my typewriter to write a story. Well and good. But getting squared away with a fresh sheet over the platen isn't the whole of it. The Happy Idea must be evolved. What if the Happy Idea does not come when I am ready for it? Happy Ideas, you know, have a disagreeable habit of hiding out. There's no hard and fast rule, that I am aware, for capturing a Happy Idea at just the moment it may be most in demand. There's lightning in a change of work, the sort of lightning that clears the air with a tonic of inspiration. When I'm paymastering the hardest I seem to be almost swamped with ideas for the story mill. Query: Will the mill grind out as good a grist if it grinds continuously? If I were sure—"

"It stands to reason," Mrs. Edwards maintained stoutly, "that if you can make $125 a month running the mill nights and Sundays, you ought to be able to make a good deal more than that with all the week days added."

"Provided," John Milton qualified, "my fountain of inspiration will flow as freely when there is nothing to hinder it as it does now when I have it turned off for twelve hours out of the twenty-four."

"Why shouldn't it?"

"I don't know, my dear," John Milton admitted, "unless it transpires that my inspiration isn't strong enough to be drawn on steadily."

"Fudge," exclaimed Mrs. Edwards.

"And then," her husband proceeded, "let us consider

another phase of the question. The demand may fall off. The chances are that it WILL fall off the moment the gods become aware of the fact that I am depending on the demand for our bread and butter. Whenever a thing becomes absolutely essential to you, Fate immediately obliterates every trail that leads to it, and you go wandering desperately back and forth, getting more and more discouraged until—"

"Until you drop in your tracks," broke in Mrs. Edwards, "and give up—a quitter."

"Quitter" is a mean word. There's something about it that jostles you, and treads on your toes.

"I don't think I'd prove a quitter," said John Milton, "even if I did get lost in a labyrinth of hard luck. It's the idea of losing you along with me that hurts."

"I'll risk *that*."

"This is a panic year," John Milton went on, "and money is hard to get. It is hardly an auspicious time for tearing loose from a regular pay-day."

John Milton and his wife lived in Chicago, and the firm for which John Milton worked had managed to keep afloat by having an account in two banks. When a note fell due at one bank, the firm borrowed from the other to pay it. Thus, by borrowing from Peter to pay Paul, and from Paul to pay Peter, the contractors juggled with their credit and kept it good. Times were hard enough in all truth, yet they were not so hard in Chicago as in other parts of the country. The World's Columbian Exposition brought a flood of visitors to the city, and a flood of cash.

"Bother the panic!" jeered Mrs. Edwards. "It won't interfere with your work. Pleasant fiction is more soothing than hard facts. People will read all the more just to forget their troubles."

"I'm pretty solid with the firm," said John Milton, veering to another tack. "I'm getting twelve hundred a year, now, with an extra hundred for taking care of the Colonel's books."

"Is there any future to it?"

"There is. I can buy stock in the company, identify myself with it more and more, and in twenty or thirty years, perhaps, move into a brownstone front on Easy street."

"No, you couldn't!" declared Mrs. Edwards.

"Why not?"

"Why, because your heart wouldn't be in your work. Ever since you were old enough to know your own mind you have wanted to be a writer. When you were twelve years old you were publishing a little paper for boys—"

"It was a four-page paper about the size of lady's handkerchief," laughed John Milton, "and it lasted for two issues."

"Well," insisted his wife, "you've been writing stories more or less all your life, and if you are ever a success at anything it will be in the fiction line. You are now twenty-six years old, and if you make your mark as an author it's high time you were about it. Don't you think so? If I'm willing to chance it, John, you surely ought to be."

"All right," was the answer, "it's a 'go.'"

And thus it was that John Milton Edwards reached his momentous decision. Perhaps you, who read these words, have been wrestling soulfully with the same question—vacillating between authorship as a vocation or as an avocation. Edwards made his decision eighteen years ago. At that time conditions were different; and it is doubtful whether, had he faced conditions as they are now, he would have decided to run his Fiction Factory on full time.

"An eye for an eye."

A writer whose stories have been used in the Munsey publications, *Pearson's* and other magazines, writes:

"How is this as an illustration of timeliness, or the personal element in writing?—I went in to see Mr. Matthew White, Jr., one day with a story and he said he couldn't read it because he had a sore eye. I had an eye for that eye as fiction, so I sat down and wrote a story in two hours' time about an editor who couldn't read any stories on account of his bum lamp, whereby he nearly missed the best story for the year. Mr. White was interested in the story mainly because he had a sore eye himself and was in full sympathy with the hero. I took the story down and read it aloud to him, selling it, of course. The story was called, "When the Editor's Eye Struck."

(Talk about making the most of your opportunities!)

The Bookman, somewhere, tells of a lady in the Middle West who caught the fiction fever and wrote in asking what price was paid for stories. To the reply that "$10 a thousand was paid for good stories" she made written response: "Why, it takes me a week to write one story, and $10 for a thousand weeks' work looks so discouraging that I guess I'd better try something else."

Poeta nascitur; non fit. This has been somewhat freely translated by one who should know, as "The poet is born; not paid."

II.
AS THE TWIG
IS BENT

Edwards' earliest attempt at fiction was a dramatic effort. The play was in three acts, was entitled "Roderigo, the Pirate Chief," and was written at the age of 12. The young playwright was Roderigo, the play was given in the loft of the Edwards barn, and twenty-five pins was the price of admission (thirty if the pins were crooked). The neighborhood suffered a famine in pins for a week after the production of the play. The juvenile element clamored to have the performance repeated, but the patrons' parents blocked the move by bribing the company with a silver dollar. It was cheaper to pay over the dollar than to buy back several thousand pins at monopoly prices.

In 1881 "Simon Girty; or, The Border Boys of the West" was offered. The first performance (which was also the last) was given in Ottawa, Kansas, and the modest fee of admission was 5 cents. The play was very favorably received and might have had an extended run had not the mothers of the "border boys" discovered that they were killing Indians with blank cartridges. Gathering in force, the mothers stormed the barn and added a realistic climax to the fourth act by spanking Simon Girty and disarming his trusty "pards."

Shortly after this, the musty records show that Edwards turned from the drama to narrative fiction, and endeavored successfully to get into print. The following, copied from an engraved certificate, offers evidence of his budding aspirations:

Frank Leslie's

BOYS' AND GIRLS' WEEKLY.

Award of Merit.

This is to certify that John Milton Edwards, Ottawa, Kansas, has been awarded Honorable Mention for excellence in literary composition. New York, Oct. 30, 1882.   FRANK LESLIE.

This "honorable mention" from the publisher of a paper, which young Edwards looked forward to from week to week and read and re-read with fascination and delight, must have inoculated him for all time with the fiction virus.   Forthwith he began publishing a story paper on a hektograph.   Saturday was the day of publication, and the office of publication was the loft of the Edwards' barn.   Even at that early day the author understood the advantage of holding "leave-offs"* in serial work.   He was altogether too successful with his leave-offs, for his readers, gasping for the rest of the story and unable to wait for the next issue of the paper, mobbed the office and forced him, with a threat of dire things, to tell them the rest of the yarn in advance of publication.   After that, of course, publication was unnecessary.

It was a problem with young Edwards, about this time, to secure enough blank paper for his scribbling needs.   Two old ledgers, only partly filled with ac-

* "Leave-off"—the place where a serial is broken, and the words "To be continued in our next" appear. Mr. Matthew White, Jr., Editor of the Argosy, is supposed to have coined the expression. At any rate, Mr. White has a great deal to do with "leave-offs" and ought to know what to call them.

counts, fell into his hands, and he used them for his callow essays at authorship. He has those ledgers now, and derives considerable amusement in looking through them. They prove that he was far from being a prodigy, and reflect credit on him for whipping his slender talents into shape for at least a commercial success in later life. Consider this:

Scene III.

J. B.—We made a pretty good haul that time, Jim.

B. J.—Yes, I'd like to make a haul like that every night. We must have got about $50,000.

J. B.—Now we will go and get our boots blacked, then go and get us a suit of clothes, and then skip to the West Indies.

Here a $50,000 robbery had been committed and the thieves were calmly discussing getting their boots blacked and replenishing their wardrobe (one suit of clothes between them seems to have been enough) before taking to flight. Shades of Sherlock, how easily a boy of 12 makes business for the police department!

Or consider this gem from Act II. The aforesaid "J. B." and "B. J." have evidently been "pinched" while getting their boots blacked or while buying their suit of clothes:

J. B.—We're in the jug at last, Jim, and I'm afraid we'll be sentenced to be shot.

B. J.—Don't be discouraged, Bill.

Enter Sleek, the detective.

Sleek.—We've got you at last, eh?

J. B.—You'll never get the money, just the same.

Sleek.—We'll shoot you if you don't tell where it is like a dog.

Then here's something else which seems to prove that young Edwards occasionally fell into rhyme:

Oh, why cut down those forests,
Our forests old and grand?

18

And oh, why cheat the Indians
    Out of all their land?
Enclosed by civilization,
    Surrounded they by towns,
Calmly when this life is done
    They seek their hunting-grounds!

John Milton Edwards has always had a place in his heart for the red man, and another for his country's vanishing timber.   He is to be congratulated on his youthful sentiments if not on the way they were expressed.

In 1882 the Edwards family removed to Chicago. There were but three in the family — the father, the mother, and John Milton. The boy was taken from the Ottawa high school and, as soon as they were all comfortably settled in the "Windy City," John Milton made what he has since believed to be the mistake of his career. His father offered him his choice of either a university or a business education. He chose to spend two years in Bryant & Stratton's Business College. His literary career would have been vastly helped had he taken the other road and matriculated at either Harvard or Yale. He had the opportunity and turned his back on it.

He was writing, more or less, all the time he was a student at Bryant & Stratton's.   The school grounded him in double-entry bookkeeping, in commercial law, and in shorthand and typewriting.

When he left the business college he found employment with a firm of subscription book publishers, as stenographer. There came a disagreement between the two partners of the firm, and the young stenographer was offered for $1,500 the retiring partner's interest. The elder Edwards, who would have had to furnish the $1,500, could not see anything alluring in the sale of books through agents, and the deal fell through. Two years later, while John Milton was working for a railroad company as ticket agent at $60 a month, his old friend of the subscription book business dropped in on him and showed him a sworn statement prepared for Dun and Bradstreet. *He had cleared $60,000 in two years!* Had John Milton bought the retiring partner's interest he would have been worth half a million before he had turned thirty.

The fiction bee, however, was continually buzzing in John Milton's brain. He had no desire to succeed at anything except authorship.

Leaving the railroad company, he went to work for a boot and shoe house as bill clerk, at $12 a week. The death of his father, at this time, came as a heavy blow to young Edwards; not only that, but it brought him heavy responsibilities and led him seriously to question the advisibility of ever making authorship—as he had secretly hoped—a vocation. His term as bill clerk was a sort of probation, allowing the young man time, in leisure hours, further to try out his talent for fiction. He was anxious to determine if he could make it a commercial success, and so justify himself in looking forward to it as a life work.

The elder Edwards had been a rugged, self-made man with no patience for anything that was not strictly "business." He measured success by an honorable standard of dollars and cents. For years previous to his death he had been accustomed to see his son industriously scribbling, with not so much as a copper cent realized from all that expenditure of energy. Naturally out of sympathy with what he conceived to be a waste of time and effort, Edwards, Sr., did not hesitate to express himself forcibly. On one ocassion he looked into his son's room, saw him feverishly busy at his desk and exclaimed, irascibly, "Damn the verses!"

Young Edwards' mother, on the other hand, was well educated and widely read; indeed, in a limited way, she had been a writer herself, and had contributed in earlier life to *Harper's Magazine*. She could see that perhaps a pre-natal influence was shaping her son's career, and understood how he might be working out his apprenticeship. Thus she became the gentle apologist, excusing the boy's unrewarded labors, on the one hand, and the father's *cui bono* ideas, on the other.

The Chicago Times, in its Sunday edition, used a story by young Edwards. It was not paid for but it was published, and the elder Edwards surreptitiously secured many copies of the paper and sent them to distant friends. Thus, although he would not admit it, he showed his pride in his son's small achievement.

From the boot and shoe house young Edwards went back to the railroad company again; from there, when the railroad company closed its Chicago office, he went to a firm of wholesalers in coke and sewer-pipe; and, later, he engaged as paymaster with the firm of contractors. Between the coke and sewer pipe and the pay-rolls he wedged in a few days of reporting for *The Chicago Morning News*; and on a certain Friday, the last of February, he got married, and was back at his office desk on the following Monday morning.

The first story for which Ewards received payment was published in *The Detroit Free Press,* Sept. 19, 1889. The payment was $8.

In April, the same year, the *Free Press* inaugurated a serial story contest. Edwards entered two stories, one under a *nom de plume*. Neither won a prize, but both were bought and published. For the first, published in 1891, he was paid $75 on Feb. 2, 1890; and for the second, published a year later, he was paid $100.

With the opening installment of the first serial the *Free Press* published a photograph of the author over a stickful of biography. On another page appeared a paragraph in boldface type announcing the discovery of a new star in the literary heavens.

The spirit of John Milton Edwards swelled within him. He feasted his eyes on his printed picture (the rapid newspaper presses had made a smudge of it), he read and re-read his lean biography (lean because not much had happened to him at that time) and he gloried over the boldface type with its message regarding the new star (he was to learn later that many similar stars are born to blush unseen) and he felt himself a growing power in the world of letters.

Verily, a pat on the back is a thing to conjure with. It is more ennobling, sometimes, than a kingly tap with a swordpoint accompanied by the words, "I dub thee knight." To the fine glow of youthful enthusiasm it opens broad vistas and offers a glimpse of glittering heights. Even though that hand-pat inspires dreams never to be realized, who shall say that a little encouragement, bringing out the best in us, does not result in much good?

And in this place John Milton Edwards would make a request of the reader of fiction. If you are pleased with a story, kindly look twice at the author's name so you may recall it pleasantly if it chances to come again under your eye. If you are a great soul, given to the scattering of benefactions, you might even go a little farther: At the expense of a postage stamp and a little time, address a few words of appreciation to the author in care of his publisher. You wist not, my beloved, what weight of gold your words may carry!

From the summer of '89 to the summer of '93 Edwards wrote many stories and sketches for *The Detroit Free Press, Puck, Truth, The Ladies' World, Yankee Blade, Frank Leslie's Popular Monthly, Chatter, Saturday Night,* and other periodicals. In 1890 he was receiving $10 a month for contributions to a little Chicago weekly called *Figaro;* and, during the same year, he found a market which was to influence profoundly a decade of work and his monetary returns; James Elverson paid him $75 for a serial to be used in *Saturday Night.*

Undoubtedly it was this serial that pointed Edwards toward the sensational story papers. A second serial, sold to *Saturday Night,* Oct. 21, 1891, brought $150; while a third, paid for July 20, 1893, netted a like amount. These transactions carried the true ring of commercial success. Apart from myth and fable, there is no more compelling siren song in history than the chink of silver. Edwards, burdened with responsibilities, gave ear to it.

The serial story, published in the *Free Press* in 1891, had made friends for Edwards. Among these friends was Alfred B. Tozer, editor of *The Chicago Ledger.* Through Mr. Tozer, Edwards received commissions for stories covering a period of years. The payment was

$1.50 a thousand words—modest, indeed, but regular and dependable.*

From 1889 to 1893 Edwards was laboring hard—all day long at his clerical duties and then until midnight in his Fiction Factory. The pay derived from his fiction output was small, (*the Ladies' World* gave him $5 for a 5,000-word story published March 18, 1890, and *The Yankee Blade* sent him $13 on Jan. 10, 1891, for a story of 8,500 words), but Edwards was prolific, and often two or three sketches a day came through his typewriter.

Early in 1893, however, he saw that he was at the parting of the ways. He could no longer serve two masters, for the office work was suffering. He realized that he was not giving the contracting firm that faithful service and undivided energy which they had the right to expect, and it was up to him to do one line of work and one only.

* In these later times, with other hands than those of Mr. Tozer at the helm, **The Chicago Ledger** seems to have become the Sargasso Sea of the popular fictionist—a final refuge for story derelicts. The craft that grows leaky and water-logged through much straining and wearisome beating about from port to port, has often and often come to anchor in the columns of the **Ledger.**

"Slips and Tips"

One of Mr. White's authors who had never been in Europe set out to write a story of a traveller who determined to get along without tipping. The author described his traveller's horrible plight while being shown around the Paris Bastille—which historic edifice had been razed to the ground some two centuries before the story was written! The author received a tip from Mr. White on his tipping story, a tip never to do it again.

24

III.
METHODS THAT
MAKE OR MAR.

Edwards has no patience' with those writers who think they are of a finer or different clay from the rest of mankind. Genius, however, may be forgiven many things, and the artistic temperament may be pardoned an occasional lapse from the conventional. This is advertising, albeit of a very indifferent sort, and advertising is a stepping-stone to success. The fact remains that True Genius does not brand with eccentricity the intelligence through which it expresses itself. The time has passed when long hair and a Windsor tie proclaim a man a favorite of the muses.

Edwards knows a young writer who believes himself a genius and who has, indeed, met with some wonderful successes, but he spoils an otherwise fine character by slovenliness of dress and by straining for a so-called Bohemian effect. Bohemia, of course, is merely a state of mind; its superficial area is fanciful and contracted; it is wildly unconventional, not to say immoral; and no right-thinking, right-feeling artist will drink at its sloppy tables or associate with its ribald-tongued habitues. The young writer here mentioned has been doped and shanghaied. As soon as he comes to himself he will escape to more creditable surroundings.

There is another writer of Edwards' acquaintance who, by profane and blasphemous utterance, seeks to convince the public that he has the divine fire. His language, it is true, shows "character," but not of the sort that he imagines.

25

A writer, to be successful, must humble himself with the lowly or walk pridefully with the great. For purposes of study he may be all things to all men, but let him see to it that he is not warped in his own self-appraisal. Never, unless he wishes to make himself ridiculous, should he build a pedestal, climb to its crest and pose. If he is worthy of a pedestal the public will see that it is properly constructed.

A writer is neither better nor worse than any other man who happens to be in trade. He is a manufacturer. After gathering his raw product, he puts it through the mill of his imagination, retorts from the mass the personal equation, refines it with a sufficient amount of commonsense and runs it into bars—of bullion, let us say. If the product is good it passes at face value and becomes a medium of exchange.

Any merchant or professional man who conducts his business with industry, taste and skill is the honorable and worthy peer of the man who writes and writes well. Every clean, conscientious calling has its artistic side and profits through the application of business principles.

Nowadays, for a writer to scribble his effusions in pale ink with a scratchy pen on both sides of a letter-sheet is not to show genius but ignorance. If he is a good manufacturer he should be proud of his product; and a good idea is doubly good if carefully clothed.

Edwards counts it a high honor that, in half a dozen editorial offices, his copy has been called "copperplate." "I always like to see one of your manuscripts come in," said Mr. White, of *The Argosy*. "Here's another of Edwards' stories," said Mr. Harriman of *The Red Book*,*

*Mr. Harriman is now with **The Ladies' Home Journal.**

"send it to the composing room just as it is." Such a condition of affairs certainly is worth striving for.

As a rule the young writer does not give this matter of neatness of manuscript the proper attention. Is he careful to count the letters and spaces in his story title and figure to place the title in the exact middle of the page? It is not difficult.

When a line is drawn between title, writer's name and the body of the story, it is easy to set the carriage pointer on "35" and touch hyphens until you reach "45." It is easy to number the pages of a manuscript in red with a bichrome ribbon, and to put the number in the middle of the sheet. Nor is it very difficult to turn out clean copy—merely a little more industry with a rubber eraser, or perhaps the re-writing of an occasional sheet.

After a manuscript is written, the number of words computed, and a publication selected wherewith to try its fortunes, a record should be made. Very early in his literary career Edwards devised a scheme for keeping track of his manuscripts. He had a thousand slips printed and bound strongly into two books of 500 slips each. Each slip consisted of a stub for the record and a form letter, with perforations so that they could easily be torn apart.

Record of Ms., No....
Title ....
Class ....
No. Words ....
Sent to......Date ....
Returned....Condition ....
Sent to......Date ....
Returned....Condition ....
Sent to......Date ....
Returned....Condition ....
Sent to......Date ....
Returned....Condition ....
Accepted ....
Am't paid......Date.......
Remarks ....
....

411 Blank Street,
    Chicago, Ill., ...189..
Editor...........
    ....
    ....
Dear Sir:
    The inclosed Ms., entitled..
....
containing about.........words,
and signed ....
is offered at your usual rates.
If not available please return.
Stamped and addressed envelope
inclosed.
      Very truly yours,
      John Milton Edwards.

Every manuscript was numbered and the numbers, running consecutively, were placed in the upper right-hand corners of the stubs. This made it easy to refer to the particular stub which held the record of a returned story.

Edwards used this form of record keeping for years. Even after he came to look upon a form letter with a manuscript as a waste of effort, he continued to use the stubs. About the year 1900 card indexes came into vogue, and now a box of cards is sufficient for keeping track of a thousand manuscripts. It is far and away more convenient than the "stub" system.

Each story has its card, and each card gives the manuscript's life history; title, when written, number of words, amount of postage required for its going and coming through the mail, when and where sent, when returned, when accepted and when paid for, together with brief notes regarding the story's vicissitudes or final good fortune. After a story is sold the card serves as a memorandum, and all these memoranda, totalled at the end of the year, form an accurate report of the writer's income.

In submitting his stories Edwards always sends the serials flat, between neatly-cut covers of tarboard girded with a pair of stout rubber bands. This makes a handy package and brings the long story to the editor's attention in a most convenient form for reading.

With double-spacing Edwards' typewriter will place 400 words on the ordinary 8 1-2 by 11 sheet. Serials of 60,000 words, covering 150 sheets, and even novelettes of half that length, travel more safely and more comfortably by express. Short stories, running up to 15—or in rare instances, to 20—pages are folded twice, inclosed in a stamped and self-addressed No. 9, cloth-lined envelope and this in turn slipped into a No. 10 cloth-lined envelope. Both these envelopes open at the end, which does not interfere with the typed superscription.

By always using typewriter paper and envelopes of the same weight, Edwards knows exactly how much postage a story of so many sheets will require.

In wrapping his serial stories for transportation by express, Edwards is equally careful to make them into neat bundles. For 10 cents he can secure enough light, strong wrapping paper for a dozen packages, and 25 cents will procure a ball of upholsterer's twine that will last a year.

Another helpful wrinkle, and one that makes for neatness, is an address label printed on gummed paper. Edwards' name and address appear at the top, following the word "From." Below are blank lines for name and address of the consignee.

In his twenty-two years of work in the fiction field Edwards has made certain of this, that there is not a detail in the preparation or recording or forwarding of a manuscript that can be neglected. Competition is keen. Big names, without big ideas back of them, are not so prone to carry weight. It's the *stuff*, itself, that counts; yet a business-like way of doing things carries a mute appeal to an editor before even a line of the manuscript has been read. It is a powerful appeal, and all on the writer's side.

Is it necessary to dwell upon the importance of a carbon copy of every story offered through the mails, or entrusted to the express companies? Edwards lost the sale of a $300 serial when an installment of the story went into a railroad wreck at Shoemaker, Kansas, and, blurred and illegible, was delivered in New York one week after another writer had written another installment to take its place. In this case the carbon copy served only as an aid in collecting $50 from the express company.

At another time, when The *Woman's Home Companion* was publishing a short serial by Edwards, one complete chapter was lost through some accident in the composing room. Upon receipt of a telegram, Edwards dug the carbon copy of the missing chapter out of his files, sent it on to New York, and presently received an extra $5 with the editor's compliments.

"My brow shall be garnished with bays."

AMERICA
Editorial Rooms, Chicago.

Aug. 16, 1889.

Dear Mr. Edwards:—

In regard to the enclosed verse, we would take pleasure in publishing it, but before doing so we beg to call your attention to the use of the word "garnish" in the last line of the first verse, and the second line of the second. The general idea of "garnish" is to decorate, or embellish. We say that a beefsteak is "garnished" with mushrooms, and so it would hardly be right to use the word in the sense of crowning a poet with a wreath of bays.

You will pardon us for calling attention to this, but you know that the most serious verse can be spoiled by by just such a slip, which of course is made without its character occurring to the mind of the writer.

Yours respectfully,
Slason Thompson & Co.

IV.
GETTING "HOOKED UP"
WITH A BIG HOUSE.

It was during the winter of 1892-3 that Edwards happened to step into the editorial office of a Chicago story paper for which he had been writing. His lucky stars were most auspiciously grouped that morning.

We shall call the editor Amos Jones. That was not his name, but it will serve.

Edwards found Jones in a very exalted frame of mind. Before him, on his desk, lay an open letter and a bundle of newspaper clippings. After greeting Edwards, Jones turned and struck the letter triumphantly with the flat of his hand.

"This," he exclaimed, "means ten thousand a year to Yours Truly!"

He was getting $50 a week as editor of the story paper, and a sudden jump from $2,600 to $10,000 a year was sufficiently unsettling to make his mood excusable. Edwards extended congratulations and was allowed to read the letter.

It was from a firm of publishers in New York City, rated up in the hundreds of thousands by the commercial agencies. These publishers, who are to figure extensively in the pages that follow, will be referred to as Harte & Perkins. They had sent the clippings to Jones, inclosed in the letter, and had requested him to use them in writing stories for a five-cent library.

Jones' enthusiasm communicated itself to Edwards. For four years the latter had been digging away, in his humble Fiction Factory, and his literary labors had brought a return averaging $25 a month. This was excellent for piecing out the office salary, but in the glow of Jones' exultation Edwards began to dream dreams.

When he left the editor's office Edwards was cogitating deeply. He had attained a little success in writing and believed that if Jones could make ten thousand a year grinding out copy for Harte & Perkins he could.

Edwards did not ask Jones to recommend him to Harte & Perkins. Jones was a good fellow, but writers are notoriously jealous of their prerogatives. After staking out a claim, the writer-man guards warily against having it "jumped." Edwards went about introducing himself to the New York firm in his own way.

At that time he had on hand a fairly well-written, but somewhat peculiar long story entitled, "The Mystery of Martha." He had tried it out again and again with various publishers only to have it returned as "well done but unavailable because of the theme." This story was submitted to Harte & Perkins. It was returned, in due course, with the following letter:

New York, March 23, 1893.

Mr. John Milton Edwards,
  Chicago, Ills.

Dear Sir:—

  We have your favor of March the 19th together with manuscript of "The Mystery of Martha," which as it is unavailable we return to you to-day by express as you request.

  We are overcrowded with material for our story paper, for which we presume you submitted this manuscript, and, indeed, we think "The Mystery of Martha" is more suitable for book publication than in any other shape.

  The only field that is open with us is that of our various five and ten cent libraries. You are perhaps familiar with these, and if you have ever done anything in this line of work, we should be pleased to have you submit the printed copy of same for our examination, and if we find it suitable we think we could use some of your material in this line.

Mr. Jones, whom you refer to in your letter, is one of our regular contributors.

Yours truly,
Harte & Perkins.

Here was the opening! Edwards lost no time in taking advantage of it and sent the following letter:

Chicago, March 25, '93.
Messrs. Harte & Perkins, Publishers,
New York City.
Gentlemen:—

I have your letter of the 23d inst. In reply would state that I have done some writing for Beadle & Adams ("*Banner Weekly*") although I have none of it at hand, at present, to send you. I also am a contributor to "*Saturday Night*," (James Elverson's paper) and have sold them a number of serial stories, receiving from them as much as $150 for 50,000 words. It is probable that material suitable to the latter periodical would be out of the question with you; still, I can write the kind of stories you desire, all I ask being the opportunity.

Inclosed please find Chapter I of "Jack o' Diamonds; or, The Cache in the Coteaux." Perhaps Western stories are bugbears with you (they are, I know, with most publishers) but there are no Indians in this one. I should like to go ahead, write this story, submit it, and let you see what I can do. I am able to turn out work in short order, if you should desire it, and feel that I can satisfy you. All I wish to know is how long you want the stories, what price is paid for them and whether there is any particular kind that you need. I have an idea that the Thrun case would afford material for a good story. At least, I think I can write you a good one with that as a foundation. Please let me hear from you.

Yours very truly,
John Milton Edwards.

To this Edwards received the following reply, under date of March 30:

We have your favor of March 25th together with small installment of story entitled "Jack o' Diamonds." Our careful reading of the installment leads us to believe that you write easily, and can probably do suitable work for our Ten-Cent

33

Library, though the particular scene described in this installment is one that can be found in almost any of the old time
libraries. It is a chestnut. A decided back number.

What we require for our libraries is something written up-
to-date, with incidents new and original, with which the daily
press is teeming. I inclose herewith a clipping headed, "Thrun
Tells it All," which, used without proper names, might suggest
a good plot for a story, and you could work in suitable action
and incident to make a good tale.

If you will submit us such a story we shall be pleased to examine same, and if found suitable we will have a place for it at
once. We pay for stories in this library $100; they should con-
tain 40,000 words, and when issued appear under our own *nom
de plume*.

Installment "Jack o' Diamonds" returned herewith.

Thus it was up to Edwards to go ahead and "make
good." Such a climax has a weird effect on some
authors. They put forth all their energy securing an
order to "go ahead" and then, at the critical moment,
experience an attack of stage fright, lose confidence
and bolt, leaving the order unfilled.

Years later, in New York, such a case came under
Edwards' observation. A young woman had besieged
a certain editor for two years for a commission. When
the coveted commission arrived, the young woman took
to her bed, so self-conscious that she was under a doctor's care for a month. The story was never turned in.

Edwards, in his own case, did not intend to put all
his eggs in one basket. He not only set to work writing
a ten-cent library story (which he called "Glim Peters
on His Mettle") but he also wrote and forwarded a
five-cent library story entitled, "Fearless Frank."
"Fearless Frank"—galloped home again bearing a request that Edwards make him over into a detective. On
April 15 Edwards received the following:

We have your favor of April 13, and note that the insurance story, relating to Thrun, is nearly completed, and will be forwarded on Monday next. I hope you have not made the hero too juvenile, as this would be a serious fault. The stories in the Ten-Cent Library are not read by boys alone but usually by young men, and in no case should the hero be a kid, such as we fear would be your idea of a Chicago newsboy.

We note that you have considered our suggestions, and also that you will fix up the "Fearless Frank" manuscript with a view of making it a detective story.

For your information, therefore, we mail you under separate cover Nos. 2, 11, 15 and 20 of the Five-Cent Library, which will give you an idea of the character of this detective. We hope you will give us what we want in both these stories.

On April 25 Edwards received a long letter that delighted him. He was "making good."

I have carefully read your story, "Glim Peters on His Mettle," and, as I feared, find the same entirely too juvenile for the Ten-Cent Library, though quite suitable for the Five-Cent Library, had it not been double the length required. I first considered the question of asking you to make two stories of it for this library, but finally decided that this would be somewhat difficult and unnecessary, as we shall find a place for it later in the columns of our *Boy's Story Paper,* to be issued under nom de plume, and will pay you $75 for same.

The chief point of merit in the story is the excellent and taking dialogue between Glim Peters, his chum and the detectives. This boy is a strong character, well delineated and natural. The incident covered by clairvoyant visits, the scene at the World's Fair and the Chinese joint experience were all excellent; but the ghost in the old Willett house, and indeed the whole plot, is poor. Judging from this story and the previous one submitted, the plot is your weak point. In future stories make no special effort to produce an unusual plot, but stick closer to the action and incident, taken as much as possible from newspapers, which are teeming with material of this character.

We shall now expect to receive from you at an early date, the detective story, and to follow this we will forward you material, in a few days, for a Ten-Cent Library story. We forward you to-day, under separate cover, several numbers to give you an idea of the class of story that is suitable for the Ten-Cent Library. Such scenes in your last story as where Glim

Peters succeeded in buying a mustang and defeated the deacon in so doing, are just the thing for the Ten-Cent Library; the same can also be said of the scene in which Meg, the girl in the bar, stands off the detectives in a vain attempt to save the villains. That is the sort of thing, and we feel that you will be able to do it when you know what we want.

I forward you, also, a copy of Ten-Cent Library No. 185, which I would like you to read, and let me know whether you could write us a number of stories for this particular series, with the same hero and the same class of incidents. If so, about how long would it take you to write 40,000 words? It is possible I may be able to start you on this series, of which we have already issued a number.

About May 1 Edwards sent the first detective story. On May 10 he received a letter, of which the following is an extract

We are in a hurry for this series (the series for the Ten-Cent Library) but after you have finished the first one, and during the time that we are reading it, you can go ahead with the second detective story, "The Capture of Keno Clark," which, although we are in no hurry for it, we may be able to use in about six weeks or two months. You did so well with the first detective story that I have no doubt you can make the second a satisfactory one. However, if we find the series for the Ten-Cent Library O. K., we will want you to write these, one after the other as rapidly as possible until we have had enough of them.

As to our method of payment, would say that it is our custom to pay for manuscripts on Thursday following the day of issue, but, agreeably with your request, we mail you a check tomorrow in payment of "Glim Peters on His Mettle," and will always be willing to accomodate you in like manner when you find it necessary to call upon us.

So Edwards made good with the publishing firm of Harte & Perkins, and for eighteen years there have been the pleasantest of business relations between them. Courteous always in their dealings, prompt in their payments to writers, and eager always to send pages and pages of helpful letters, Harte & Perkins have grown to be the most substantial publishers in the country. Is it because of their interest in their writers? Certainly not in spite of it!

For them Edwards has written upwards of five hundred five-cent libraries, a dozen or more serials for their story paper, many serials for their boys' weekly, novelettes for their popular magazines, and a large number of short stories. For these, in the last eighteen years, they have paid him more than $35,000.

Nor, during this time, was he writing for Harte & Perkins exclusively. He had other publishers and other sources of profit.

As an instance of helpfulness that did not help, Edwards once attempted to come to the assistance of Howard Dwight Smiley. Smiley wrote his first story, and Edwards sent it on to *The Argosy* with a personal letter to Mr. White. Such letters, at best, can do no more than secure for an unknown writer a little more consideration than would otherwise be the case; they will not warp an editor's judgment, no matter how warmly the new writer is recommended. The story came back with a long letter of criticism and with an invitation for Smiley to try again. He tried and tried, perhaps a dozen times, and always the manuscript was returned to the patient Smiley by the no less patient editor. At last Smiley wrote a story about a tramp who became entangled with a cyclone. The "whirler," it seems, had already picked up the loose odds and ends of a farm yard, along with a churnful of butter. In order to escape from the cyclone, Smiley's tramp greased himself with the butter from the churn and slid out of the embrace of the twisting winds. "Chuck it," said Edwards; "I'm surprised at you, Smiley." Smiley did "chuck it"— but into a mail-box, addressed to Mr. White, and Mr. White "chucked" a check for $12 right back for it! Whereupon Smiley chuckled inordinately—and came no more to Edwards for advice.

V.

NICKEL THRILLS AND
DOLLAR SHOCKERS.

The word "sensational" as applied to fiction has been burdened with an opprobrium which does not rightfully belong to it. Ignorance and prejudice and hypocrisy have conspired to defame a very worthy word.

Certain good but misguided people will turn shudderingly from a nickel novel and complacently look for thrills in a "best seller." Often and often the "best seller" is to be had for 95 cents or $1 at the department stores. Not infrequently it spills more blood than the nickel thriller, but the blood is spilled on finer paper, and along with it are idealized pictures of heroine and hero done by the best artists.

As a matter of course the dollar dreadful is better done. The author probably took six months or a year to do it, and if it is well advertised and proves a success he reaps a modest fortune. On the other hand, the nickel novel is written in three days or a week and brings the author $50. Why shouldn't the dollar book show a higher grade of craftmanship? But is it less vicious than the novel that sells for five cents? To draw the matter still finer, is either form of fiction vicious?

If we turn to Webster and seek a definition of "sensational" we find: "Suited or intended to excite temporarily great interest or emotion; melodramatic; emotional."

This does not mean that sensational writing is vicious writing. It is wrong to classify as vicious or degrading

38

the story of swift action and clean ethics, or to compare it with that prurient product of the slums which deals with problems of sex.

The tale that moves breathlessly but logically, that is built incident upon incident to a telling climax with the frankly avowed purpose to entertain, that has no questionable leanings or immoral affiliations—such a tale speeds innocently an idle hour, diverts pleasantly the harrassed mind, freshens our zeal for the duties of life, and occasionally leaves us with higher ideals.

We are all dreamers. We must be dreamers before we are doers. If some of the visions that come to us in secret reverie were flaunted in all their conceit and inconsistency before the world, not one of us but would be the butt of the world's ridicule. And yet, out of these highly tinted imaginings springs the impulse that carries us to higher and nobler things.

A difference in the price of two commodities does not necessarily mark a moral difference in the commodities themselves. *The Century Magazine* sells for 35 cents, while *The Argosy* sells for 10 cents. You will be told that *The Century* is "high class" and with a distinct literary flavor, perhaps that it is more elevating. Even so; yet which of these magazines is doing more to make the world really livable? Ask the newsdealer in your town how many *Centuries* he sells, and how many *Argosies.*

Readers are not made for the popular magazines, but the popular magazines are made for the people. Unless there was a distinct and insistent demand for this sort of entertainment, so many all-story magazines, priced at a dime, could not exist.

Nickel thrillers cater largely to a juvenile clientele. Taking them by and large—there are a few exceptions, of course—they are as worthy of readers as the dime magazines; and many a serial in a dime magazine has been republished in cloth and made into a "best seller."*

Why is it that, if a lad in his teens robs a jewelry store and is apprehended, almost invariably the newspaper report has a bundle of nickel libraries found in his pocket? Why a nickel library and not a "yellow" newspaper?

The standard of judgment which places a nickel novel in the heart-side pocket of the young degenerate, harks back to a period when "yellow-back" literature was really vicious; it is a judgment by tradition, unsupported by present-day facts. The world moves, and as it moves it grows constantly better. Reputable publishers of cheap fiction have elevated the character of their output until now some of the weekly stories they publish are really admirable; in many instances they are classics.

A few years ago, at a convention of Sunday School teachers at Asbury Park, N. J., a minister boldly praised the "Diamond Dick" stories. He declared that while action rattled through the pages of these tales like bullets from a Gatling, he had found nothing immoral in them, nothing suggestive, nothing to deprave. The lawless received their just reward and virtue emerged triumphant. It was his thought that a few "Diamond Dick" stories might, with benefit, take the place, in Sunday School libraries, of the time-honored book in which

* "Dan Quixote," for instance published in **The All-Story Magazine,** and republished as "The Brass Bowl."

the boy goes a-fishing on Sunday and falls into the river.

One of the "Frank Merriwell" stories tells of a sensitive, shrinking lad at an academy who was hazed into a case of pneumonia from which he died. The hero breaks the news of the boy's death to his widowed mother and comforts her in her bereavement. From beginning to end the story is told with a sympathy, and such a thorough understanding of boy-nature, that the hold on the juvenile reader is as strong as the theme is uplifting.

This is not "trash." It is literature sold at a price which carries it everywhere, and the result is untold good.

The fact remains, however, that not every publisher of nickel novels has so high a standard. The paternal eye, in overseeing the fiction of the young, must be discriminating. Blood-and-thunder has had its day; but, if the rising generation is not to be a race of mollycoddles, care must be exercised in stopping short of the other extreme.

The life of today sets a pattern for the fiction of today. The masses demand rapid-fire action and good red brawn in their reading matter. Their awakened moral sense makes possible the muck-raker; and when they weary of the day's evil and the day's toil, it is their habit to divert themselves with pleasant and exciting reading. And it must be CLEAN.

VI.

MAKING GOOD

BY HARD WORK.

With the beginning of the year 1894 Edwards was
learning the knack of the nickel novel and its ten-cent
brother, and making good with his New York publishers.
During 1893 the work he turned in was of fair quality,
but he was not satisfied with that and labored to improve. Each succeeding story came nearer and nearer
the high mark. Believing that whatever is worth doing
is worth doing well, he was constantly asking himself,
"How can I make my next story better than the one I
have just finished?" The publishers helped him. Every
manuscript submitted was read personally by Mr. Perkins, and brought a letter dissecting the story and stating
which incidents were liked, and why, and which incidents were not liked, and why. Edwards feels that he
can never be sufficiently grateful to Mr. Perkins for
this coaching in the gentle art of stalking a reader's
elusive interest.

Had Edwards remained a paymaster in the employ
of the contracting firm, he would have received $1,200
for his services in 1893. He severed his connection
with his paymaster's salary in June, and at the end of
the year his Fiction Factory showed these results:

4	Five-Cent Library stories at $50 each........$	200.
1	Juvenile serial	100.
1	Juvenile serial	75.
13	Ten-Cent Library stories at $100. each........	1300.
1	Serial for Saturday Night	150.

Total ....$ 1825.

In other words, Edwards had taken out of his Fiction Factory $625 more than his salary as paymaster would have amounted to for the year. He felt vastly relieved, and his wife laughingly fell back on her woman's prerogative of saying "I told you so." This was a good beginning, and Edwards felt sure that he would be able to do even better during 1894. He was coming along splendidly with the Ten-Cent Library work. On Jan. 30 Mr. Perkins paid this tribute to his growing powers:

"I have just finished reading your story, "Dalton's Double," which I find to be as good as anything you have given us. I must compliment you upon the varied incident which you cram into these stories, of a nature that is well suited to them."

It was Edwards' custom to forward a Ten-Cent Library story every two weeks, and there were months in which he wrote three stories, taking ten days for each one. As these stories were 40,000 words in length, three in thirty days were equivalent to 120,000 words.

During 1893 he wrote his stories twice: first a rough draft and then the printer's copy. In 1894 he began making his first copies clean enough for the compositor. Had he not done this he could never have accomplished such a large amount of work.

On April 10, when everything was going swimmingly and he was taking in $300 a month for the library work, he was brought up short in his career of prosperity. Mr. Perkins wrote him to finish the story upon which he was engaged and then to stop the library work until further orders. It had been decided to use "re-prints" in the series. This could very easily be done as the Library had been published for years and some of the earlier stories could be brought out again without injuring the sale. The letter, which was a profound disappointment to Edwards, closed as follows:

"I regret the necessity of curtailing your work, for I am entirely satisfied with it, and if we did not find it necessary to adopt the measure referred to above, with a view to decreasing expenses during the summer months and dull season, I should have wished to have you continue right along. I have no doubt that you will be able to find a place for your material in the meantime."

This fell upon Edwards like a bolt from a clear sky. He began to regret his "paymaster crutch" and to imagine dire things. He had been giving his time almost exclusively to Harte & Perkins, and had lost touch with publications for which he had been writing previous to 1893. Where, he asked himself, was he to place his material in the meantime?

There is little sentiment in business. Harte & Perkins, whenever they find a line of work is not paying, will cut it off at an hour's notice, by telegraph if necessary. The man receiving the telegram, of course, can only make the best of it. This is a point which Edwards has always disliked about the work for publishers of this class of fiction: the writer, no matter how prosperous he may be at any given time, is always in a state of glorious uncertainty.

But Edwards fell on his feet. It so happened that he had sent to Harte & Perkins, some time before, copies of *Saturday Night* containing two of his stories. He had done this in the attempt to prove to them that he could write for *The Weekly Guest,* their story paper. This little incident shows how important it is for a writer to get as many anchors to windward as possible.

Eight days after being cut off from the library work, Edwards received a letter from Mr. Harte. Mr. Perkins had left New York on business, but had turned over the printed work in *Saturday Night* for Mr. Harte's inspection before leaving. Mr. Harte wrote, in part:

"I like your work in *Saturday Night,* and think we shall be able to give you a commission for a *Weekly Guest* story, provided you can lend yourself successfully to our suggestions as to style, etc., and give us permission to publish under any of the pen names we use in the office.

We want a story of the Stella Edwards type. We send you to-day one or two samples of the class of work desired, so that you may be able to see just what it is. If you can do the work, we shall be pleased to send you a title and plot, with synopsis. You can then write us two installments for a trial, and, if satisfactory, I have no doubt we could arrange to give you a quantity of work in this line.

I feel, after reading the samples you submitted, that you will be able to meet our requirements in this class of story. The two stories we send you are the work of a masculine pen, and though not so easy to lose one's identity in literary work, this class of story does not seem to present the ordinary difficulties; at least, that is the testimony of our authors who have tried it."

Edwards was booked to attempt a gushing love story, to follow a copy and make it appear as though a woman had done the writing! Quite a jump this, from a rapid-fire Ten-Cent Library story for young men to a bit of sentimental fiction for young women. However, he went at it, and he went at it with a determination to make good. It was either that or go paymastering again.

On April 24 he received title, synopsis and plot of "Bessie, the Beautiful Blind Girl," and began charging himself with superheated sentiment preparatory to beginning his work. The popular young lady authoress, "Stella Edwards," whose portrait in a decollete gown had been so often flaunted in the eyes of "her" public, was a myth. The "stuff" supposedly written by the charming "Stella Edwards" was ground out by men who

were versatile enough to befool women readers, with a
feminine style. Edwards, it transpired, was able to do
this successfully for a time, but ultimately he failed to
round off the rough corners of a style too decidedly
masculine for "Miss Edwards." But this is anticipating.

On May 3 he had sent the two trial installments, and
from New York came the word:

"We like the two opening installments of 'Bessie, the Beautiful Blind Girl.' The style is good, the action brisk and sensational and of a curiosity-arousing character.

It is our belief that you are capable of presenting a desirable variation from the former Stella Edwards' stories, by introducing romantic incidents of a novel and more exalted character.

In most of the other Stella Edwards' yarns there was little
plot and the action was rarely varied. The action comprised the
pursuit and capture, the recapture and loss of the heroine, she
being constantly whirled, like a shuttle-cock, from the hero to
the villian, then to the female villian, then back again to the
hero for a few tantalizing moments, and so on to the end.

You can readily improve upon this by introducing scenes a
little more fresh, and far more interesting.

It is about time for Stella to improve, and we believe you
are just the man to make her do better work.

Go on with the story and force our readers to exclaim,
'Well, that's the best story Stella has written!'"

While Edwards was deep in the sorrows of "Bessie,
the Beautiful Blind Girl," he received from his publishers on May 10 orders which hurled him headlong into
another "Stella Edwards" yarn.

"Owing to a change in our publishing schedule of Guest
stories, it will be necessary to anticipate the issue of 'Bessie, the
Beautiful Blind Girl' by another story of the same type, sixteen
installments, same as the one you are now working on. The
title of this new story will be 'The Bicycle Belle,' and will deal
with the bicycle as the matter of central interest in the first installment or two. I send you a synopsis of the story prepared by
one of our editors. This will simply give you an idea of one
way of developing the theme. It does not, however, suit our
plans, and we will ask you to invent something quite different."

Always and ever Harte & Perkins kept their fingers on the pulse of their reading pubilc. The safety bicycle was the fashion, in those days, and Harte & Perkins were usually first to exploit a fashion or a fad in their story columns. Whenever they had a story with a particularly popular and striking theme, it was their habit to flood the country with sample copies of *The Weekly Guest*, breaking off a generous installment of the serial in such a breathless place that the reader was forced to buy succeding issues of the *Guest* in order to get the rest of the story. So that is what the change in their publishing schedule meant. They wanted to boom the circulation of the *Guest* with a bicycle story.

Edwards shelved Bessie the beautiful at the 7th installment and threw himself into the tears, fears and chivalry of "The Bicycle Belle." This was on May 12. Three days later, on May 15, he forwarded two installments of the bicycle story for Harte & Perkins' inspection. On May 16, before these installments had reached the publishers, Edwards was requested as follows:

"As we shall not be able to begin, in the Guest, your story, 'Bessie, the Beautiful Blind Girl,' until after January the first, next, it will be well to change the scene to a winter setting. This can be very easily done in the two installments that we have on hand, if you will make a note of it and keep it up for the balance of the story. In the first installment we will show the girl leaping into the river with a few cakes of ice floating about, and in the scene where she is expelled from the house there will be plenty of snow. It will make a more effective picture and be more seasonable for the story."

More trouble! Harte & Perkins had two installments, and did not seem to know that Edwards had five more installments on hand, pending the completion of the bicycle yarn. But he was ready to turn summer into winter, or day into night, in order to make good. On May 18 he received a report on the two installments of the bicycle story.

"The two installments of 'The Bicycle Belle' have been read and approved by our editor, who says that the story opens very well, with plenty of animated action, briefly yet graphically pictured. You seem to have caught our idea exactly, and we would be pleased to have you go ahead with the story, finishing it before you again take up 'Bessie, the Beautiful Blind Girl.' "

On June 3 Edwards sent installments three to sixteen of the bicycle story, which was the complete manuscript. Ten days later he was informed:

" 'The Bicycle Belle' is crowded with dramatic action and is just what we want. In the next it would be well to have a little more of the female element just to demonstrate that 'Stella Edwards' is up-to-date."

None the less pleasant was this news, contained in a letter dated June 18:

"We have placed to your credit, upon our books, the sum of three hundred dollars in payment for 'The Bicycle Belle,' which will be the figure for all this class of stories from your pen which are accepted for *The Weekly Guest.*"

Up to that time this was the most money Edwards had ever received for a serial story, and very naturally he felt elated. Under date of June 20 he wrote Harte & Perkins and told them that he was planning a trip East as soon as he had finished with "Bessie, the Beautiful Blind Girl." He received a cordial invitation from the publishers to come on as soon as possible as they had something which they particularly wanted him to do for them.

The story of the blind girl was forwarded on June 30. A flaw was discovered in it and several installments were returned for correction—not a serious flaw, indeed, but one which necessitated a little revision. The revision made, the story passed at once to acceptance.

In July Edwards was in New York and called personally upon Harte & Perkins. He found them pleasant and capable gentlemen—all that his fancy had pictured them through months of correspondence. Inasmuch as it was Edwards' first visit to the metropolis, he studied the city with a view to using it in some of his fiction.

The special work which Mr. Harte wanted Edwards to do for the firm was a story of which he gave the salient features. It was to be written in the best Archibald Clavering Gunter style.

As Edwards had imitated successfully the mythical "Stella Edwards," he was now confronted with the more trying task of imitating the style of a popular living author. He read Gunter from "Barnes of New York" down; and then, when completely saturated with him, turned off two installments of "The Brave and Fair" and sent them on. He was visiting in Michigan, at the time, and a letter under date of August 20, reached him while he was still in that state.

"I have just finished reading the two installments of 'The Brave and Fair.' I think you have made a very good opening indeed. It reads smoothly and seems to me to be very much in Gunter's light narrative style, which is what we are after. It remains to be seen whether you can get as close to Gunter in what might be called his tragedy vein as opposed to the comedy vein, which you have successfully worked up in these two installments."

"The Brave and Fair," going forward to the publishers piece by piece, seemed to arouse their enthusiasm. "We have read up to installment eight. It is fine! Full of heroic action! Bristling with exciting scenes!" When the completed manuscript was in the publishers' hands, on October 20, there came another compliment-ary letter.

" 'The Brave and Fair' bristled with exciting action to the close.

The best incidents in it are those descriptive of Chub Jones' heroic self-sacrifice. In our opinion, this stands out as the gem of the story, because it makes the reader's heart bound with ad-miration for the little hero."

Hundreds of thousands of sample copies of *The Weekly Guest,* with first chapters of this story, were scattered all over the land. Later, the book was issued in paper covers. Harte & Perkins paid the author $500 for the story, then ordered another of the same type for which he was given $450.

These stories were written under a *nom de plume* which Harte & Perkins had copyrighted. The *nom de plume* was their property and could not be appropriated by any other publisher. Edwards wrote three of the yarns, and a friend of his wrote others.

All the year Edwards had been patted on the back. On Dec. 14 came a blow between the eyes. He had been commissioned to write another "Stella Edwards" rhapsody, but was overconfident and did not take time to surround himself with the proper "Stella Edwards" atmosphere. Two installments went forward, and this letter came back:

"I have just finished reading 'Two Hearts Against the World.' I regret to say that the story will not do, and it would be as well for you not to attempt to remodel it. In other words, the way you are handling the subject is not satisfactory to us and is not a question of minor detail. We shall be obliged to give this work into other hands to do. The story, as far as it goes, is wildly improbable and has a lack of cohesion in the in-cident. I think you wrote it hurriedly, and without mature thought. These stories have to seem probable even if they deal with unusual events."

There was bitterness in that, not so much because Edwards had lost $300 but because he had failed to make good. His pride suffered more than his pocket. Later, however, he wrote some more "Stella Edwards" stories for Harte & Perkins and they were highly praised; but that type of fiction was not his forte.

The year 1894 closed with Harte & Perkins giving Edwards a chance at a new five-cent weekly they were starting. It was merely a shift from *The Weekly Guest* back to the libraries again.

His work for Harte & Perkins, during the year, showed as follows:

```
10 Ten-Cent Libraries at $100 each ...........$ 1000.
Two "Stella Edwards" stories at $300 each....   600.
"The Brave and Fair" ........................   500.
"The Man from Montana".......................   450.
2 Five-Cent Libraries at $50 each ...........   100.
1 Juvenile serial ...........................   100.

    Total ...................................$2,750.
```

The work tabulated above approximates 850,000 words, and takes no account of work sold to other publishers. By industry alone Edwards had secured a fair income.

W. Bert Foster, a friend of Edwards', who for twenty-five years has kept a story-mill of his own busily grinding with splendid success, has this to say about a slip he once made in his early years:

"When I was a young writer I sold a story to a juvenile paper. It was published. And not until the boys began to write in about it did either the editor or I discover that I had my hero dying of thirst *on a raft in Lake Michigan!*"

VII.

INSPIRATION

ALIAS INDUSTRY.

Jack London advises authors not to wait for inspiration but to "go after it with a club." Bravo! It is not intended, of course, to lay violent hands on the Happy Idea or to knock it over with a bludgeon. Mr. London realizes that, nine times out of ten, Happy Ideas are drawn toward industry as iron filings toward a magnet. The real secret lies in making a start, even though it promises to get you nowhere, and inspiration will take care of itself.

There's a lot of "fiddle-faddle" wrapped up in that word "inspiration." It is the last resort of the lazy writer, of the man who would rather sit and dream than be up and doing. If the majority of writers who depend upon fiction for a livelihood were to wait for the spirit of inspiration to move them, the sheriff would happen along and tack a notice on the front door—while the writers were still waiting.

More and more Edwards' experience, and the experience of others which has come under his observation, convinces him that inspiration is only another name for industry. When he was paymaster for the firm of contractors, he went to the office at 8 o'clock in the morning, took half an hour for luncheon at noon, and left for home at half-past 5. When he broke away from office routine, he promised himself that he would give as much, or more, of his time to his Fiction Factory.

What he feared was that ideas would fail to come, and that he would pass the time sitting idly at his typewriter. In actual practice, he found it almost uncanny how the blank white sheet he had run into his machine invited ideas to cover it. After five, ten or fifteen minutes of following false leads, he at last hit upon the right scent and was off at a run. With every leap his enthusiasm grew upon him. A bright bit of dialogue would evoke a chuckle, a touch of pathos would bring a tear, an unexpected incident shooting suddenly out of the tangled threads would fill him with rapture, and for the logical but unexpected climax he reserved a mood like Caesar's, returning from the wars and celebrating a triumph.

In the ardor of his work he forgot the flight of time. He balked at leaving his typewriter for a meal and went to bed only when drowsiness interfered with his flow of thought.

Whether he was writing a Five-Cent Library, a serial story or a novel which he hoped would bring him fame and fortune, the same delight filled him whenever he achieved a point which he knew to be worth while. And whenever such a point is achieved, my writer friend, there is something that rises in your soul and tells you of it in words that never lie.

No matter what you are writing, unless you can thrill to every detail of excellence in what you do, unless you can worry about the obscure sentence or the unworthy incident until they are sponged out and recast, it is not too much to say that you will never succeed at the writing game. Love the work for its own sake and it will bring its inspiration and its reward; look upon it as a grind and melancholy failure stalks in your wake.

There can be no inspiration without industry, and no industry without inspiration. Start your car on the batteries of industry and it will soon be running on the magneto of inspiration. Drive yourself to your work, and presently interest will be aroused and your eager energies will need a curb instead of a spur.

Edwards has written two 30,000-word stories a week for months at a time; he has written one 30,000-word story and one 40,000-word serial in one week; he has begun a Five Cent Library story at 7 o'clock in the morning and worked the clock around, completing the manuscript at 7 the next morning; and he has done other things that were possible only because industry brought inspiration, and inspiration takes no account of time.

Edwards knows a writer of short stories who is like a crazy man for days while he is frantically groping for an idea. When the idea comes, he figuratively sweats blood for a week in pulling it through his typewriter; and then, when the story is in the mails, he takes to his bed for a week from physical exhaustion. Result: Three weeks, one story, and anywhere from $50 to $75. He is conscientious, but his method is wrong. Instead of storming through the house and tearing his hair while the idea eludes him, he should roll in a fresh sheet, sit calmly down in front of the keys, look out of the window or around the room and start off with the first object that appeals to him.

There are writers who will have a Billikin for inspiration, or some other fetich that takes the place of a Billikin. Edwards has an elephant tobacco-jar that has occasionally helped him. Sometimes it is a pipeful of the elephant's contents, and sometimes it is merely a long look at the elephant that starts the psychology to working.

Of course it isn't really the Billikin, or the elephant, or the tobacco that does the trick. They merely enable us to concentrate upon the work in hand: from them we gather hope that work will produce results, so we get busy and results come.

The main thing is to break the shackles of laziness and begin our labors; then, after that, to forget that we are laboring in the sheer joy of creation with which our labor inspires us.

New York, Sept. 2, 1911.
My dear Mr. Edwards:
You fairly have me stumped. With the greatest pleasure in the world I would give you what you ask for your book, but I am not certain that I can recall any humorous anecdotes; and as for"quips," I look the word up and discover that it means: "A sneering or mocking remark; gibe; taunt." And I am afraid I am not equal to evolving any of these . . . . All I can recall now is that in my early days an editor of the *New York Herald* wanted to kick me down the editorial stairs because I asked pay for amusement notes they had been printing for nothing. I fled, leaving my last Ms. behind me—which they also printed gratis. Now this wasn't humorous to anybody at the time, and if there was any 'quip,' that editor uttered it, and I don't remember now just the language he used.

Very truly yours,
Matthew White, Jr.,
Editor *The Argosy*.

VIII.

THE WOLF ON

THE SKY-LINE.

For Edwards, the year 1895 dawned in a blaze of prosperity and went out in the gathering shadows of impending disaster.

Spring found him literally swamped with orders, and he tried the experiment of hiring a young man stenographer and typist to assist him. The young man was an expert in his line and proved so efficient an aide that Edwards hired another who was equally proficient. Two stenographers failing to help him catch up with his flood of orders, he secured a third.

One assistant put in his time copying manuscripts and cataloguing clippings, to another the library work was dictated, and the third was employed on "Stella Edwards" material.

Edwards was versatile, and he experienced no difficulty in passing from one class of work to another. He was able to chronicle the breathless adventures of the hero of the Five-Cent Library to one stenographer, then turn to the other and dictate two or three chapters of a serial of the class written by Laura Jean Libby, and then fill in the gaps between dictation with altogether different work on his own machine.

Although Edwards kept these three stenographers for several months, and although he has since frequently availed himself of the services of an amanuensis, yet he is free to confess that he doubts the expediency of such help. Successful dialect cannot be wrapped up in a stenographer's "pothooks," and so much dialect was used in the library stories that the young man at work on them had to familiarize himself with the contorted forms and write them down from memory. It took him so long to do this, and required so much of Edwards' time making corrections, that the profit on his work was disappointing.

With such an office force grinding out copy, during the early months of 1895 the Fiction Factory was a very busy place. During January and February the cash returns amounted to $1,500. This, Edwards discovered later, was no argument in favor of stenographer assistance, for he has since, working alone, earned upward of $1,000 in a month.

In February Edwards was requested by Harte & Perkins to submit a story for a new detective library which they were starting, and of which they were very choice. The work was as different as possible from the two or three detective yarns Edwards had written in 1893. He wrote and submitted the story, and Mr. Perkins' criticisms are given below by way of showing how carefully the stories were examined. The letter from which the excerpt is taken was written Feb. 13, 1895. The mythical detective, who has become known throughout the length and breadth of the land, shall here be referred to as "Joe Blake."

"There is one point to which I would call your attention. On page 5, Chapter II opens in this way: 'A young man to see Dr. Reynolds; no card.' Joe Blake, otherwise 'Dr. Reynolds,' told the boy to show the visitor in. The place was Chicago. Scene in room in prominent hotel the second day after Joe

Blake had had an interview with Abner Larkin, 9 o'clock in the evening.'

This is too trite and not easily expressed. Such references to time, place, etc., impress the reader with the fact that he is reading a romance and not a real story of Joe Blake's experiences. This particular point should be kept in mind. We want these stories to appear as natural as possible.

In the opening of the installment, where Mr. Larkin presents himself to Joe, you have duplicated the common-place method of most writers. There should be more originality in the way Joe Blake's attention is called to various cases and not a continual repetition of calls at his office, which, though natural enough, become tiresome to the reader. In this same opening there is not enough detective flavor, and here, as well as in other places, Joe does not appear to be the man of authority, which he is usually found to be. These are little things, but I believe if you will take care of them they will help the story greatly."

This will illustrate the care with which Harte & Perkins looked over the manuscripts submitted to them, to the end that they might be made to reflect their ideas of what good manuscripts should be. If a writer could not do their work the way they wanted it done he was not long in getting his *conge*. In the case of the story mentioned above, it was returned, rewritten, and made to conform to Mr. Perkins' ideas.

On Jan. 9 Harte & Perkins had written Edwards:

"It is more than apparent that the library business is not very flourishing, and hereafter we shall only be able to pay $40 for these stories. I think this will be satisfactory to you, for I know you can do this class of work very rapidly."

This meant a loss of $10 a week, and Edwards endeavored to make up for it by increasing his output. Particularly he wanted a chance to write another "Stella Edwards" story, just to show the firm that he could do the work. Mr. Harte gave him an order for the serial, stating that the new story was to follow "The Bicycle

58

Belle," then running in *The Weekly Guest*. The story was to be in twelve installments of 5,250 words each, totalling some 63,000 words. For this Edwards was to receive $200. This hint was given him:

"Have plenty of romance, without too great extravagance, and make sure of at least one wedding and that in the beginning of the story."

With the order came a picture which it was desired to use in illustrating the opening installment. Edwards was to write the installment around the picture. He completed the story, called it "Little Bluebell," and received the following commendation after two installments had been received and read:

"I have just finished reading the first two installments of your story, 'Little Bluebell,' and I have to say that the same is entirely satisfactory, unquestionably the best thing you have given us in this line of work."

Although he was turning out Five-Cent Libraries, Stella Edwards serials, short sketches for *Puck* and stories for other publishers than Harte & Perkins, Edwards was constantly on the alert for more work in order to keep his stenographers busy. He asked Mr. Perkins for orders for the Ten-Cent Library, and for juvenile serials for the boys' paper. He was allowed to send in some "Gentlemen Jim" stories for the dime publication. The pay was not munificent, however, being only $50 for 37,000 words.

The "Little Bluebell" story was followed by another "Stella Edwards" serial entitled "A Weird Marriage." This yarn hit the bull's-eye with a bang. In fact, it was said to be the best thing ever done by "Stella Edwards." And then, after scoring these two successive hits, Edwards tripped on a third story called "Beryl's Lovers," and he fell so hard that it was ten years before the firm ever asked him to do any more writing in that line.

In the Fall of 1895 Edwards discovered that he had been working too hard. A doctor examined his lungs, declared that he was threatened with tuberculosis and ordered him to the Southwest. In November he and his wife left Chicago, Edwards carrying with him his typewriter and a plentiful supply of typewriter paper. He transformed a stateroom in the compartment sleeper into his Fiction Factory, finishing two installments of the ill-fated "Beryl's Lovers" while enroute.

These installments, forwarded from Phoenix, Arizona, by express, went into a wreck at Shoemaker, Kansas, and were delivered to Harte & Perkins, torn and illegible, two weeks after the story had been taken over by another writer. Edwards filed a claim against the express company for $300, and then compromised for $50—all the express people were liable for by the terms of their receipt.

From November, 1895, until April, 1896, Edwards was located on a ranch near Phoenix, Arizona, writing Five-Cent Libraries for Harte & Perkins and sketches and short stories for other publishers. His health was steadily declining, and he could bring himself to his work only by a supreme effort of the will and at the expense of much physical torture. In May, 1896, he was told that he must get farther away from the irrigated districts around Phoenix and into the arid hills. To this end he interested himself in a gold mine, and went East to form a company and secure the necessary capital to purchase and develop it.

About the middle of July he returned to Phoenix, still writing but hoping for golden rewards from the mining venture which would ultimately make his writing less of a business and more of a pastime.

His health continued to decline and he was ordered to give up writing entirely and exercise constantly in the open. He at once telegraphed Harte & Perkins to this effect. On Oct. 13 they wrote:

"We have heard nothing from you since receipt of your telegram to take all work out of your hands. This, of course, we attended to at once, but on your account, as well as our own, we were very sorry to learn that you found it necessary to give up the work, and trust that the illness from which you are suffering will not be lasting.....If, in future, you should be able to write again, we shall try to find a place for your work."

So the old firm and Edwards parted for a time. A few weeks proved the mining venture a failure, and $10,-000 which Edwards had put away out of the profits of his writing had vanished—gone to make the failure memorable. Nor had his health returned.

In some desperation, just before New Year's of '97, Mr. and Mrs. Edwards entrained for New York, Edwards pinning his hopes to Harte & Perkins. He had less than $100 to his name when he and his wife reached the metropolis.

One hundred dollars will not carry a man and his wife very far in New York, even when both are in good health and the man can work. Ambition alone kept Edwards alive and gave him hope for the future.

The Factory out-put for 1895:

3	Five-Cent Libraries at $50 each ....$	150.
29	Five-Cent Libraries at $40 each............	1160.
2	Detective stories at $40 each	80.

2	Ten-Cent Library stories at $50 each........	100.
	"Little Bluebell," serial	200.
	"A Weird Marriage,"	300.
		$ 1990.
	Detroit Free Press, Contributions	22.
	Total ....$ 2012.	

For 1896:

24	Five-Cent Libraries at $40 each ....$	960.
	Short fiction	71.50
	Total ....$ 1031.50	

For cold brutality perhaps the rejection slip worded as below is unequalled:

We are sorry to return your paper, but you have written on it.

Respectfully yours,
The Editor.

Before Mr. Karl Edwin Harriman, of The Red Book, had ventured into the editorial end of the writing trade, he wrote an article on an order from a certain Eastern magazine. Later, that magazine decided that it could not use the article, although it had been paid for, and, with Mr. Harriman's permission, turned it over to an agent to market elsewhere.

The agent, not knowing Mr. Harriman had associated himself with a certain magazine, sent the manuscript to that publication, in the ordinary way.

It was up to Mr. Harriman, then, to consider it in an editorial capacity. He was unable to purchase the manuscript, and returned it to the agent with a reproof for having submitted such an article. and indicating that the author had a great deal to learn before he could feel justified in seeking a market among the best known magazines.

IX.

RAW MATERIAL

Where does the writer get his plot-germs, the raw material which he puts through the mill of his fancy and finally draws forth as a finished and salable product? Life is a thing of infinite variety, and the plot-germ is a thing of Life or it is nothing. Being a mere basic suggestion of the story, the germs must come from the author's experience, or from the experiences of others which have been brought to his attention. Unconsciously the germ lodges in his mind, and his ingenuity, handling other phases of existence, works out the completed plot.

It follows that the richer an author's experience and the more ardent his imagination the better will be the plot evolved, providing his fine sense of values has been adequately cultivated. But no matter how adventurous and varied a personal experience, or how warm the fancy, or how highly cultivated the mind in its adaptation of fact to fiction, the experience of others compels attention if a writer's work is to be anything more than self-centered.

Newspapers, chronicling the everyday events of human existence, have not only suggested countless successful plot-germs but have likewise helped in the rounding out of the plot. An editor wrote Edwards, as long ago as March 30, 1893: "What we require in our stories is something written up to date, with incidents new and original. The daily press is teeming with this raw material.'' This fact is universally recognized, so that very few authors neglect to avail themselves of this source of inspiration.

As a case in point, a few years ago one noted author was accused of appropriating the work of another noted author. Plagiarism was seemingly proved by evoking the aid of the deadly parallel. Nevertheless the evidence was far from being conclusive. Each author had done no more than build a similar story upon the same newspaper clipping! Neither was in the wrong. No one writer has a monopoly of the facts of life, or of the right to use those facts as they filter through columns of the daily press.

Fortunately for Edwards, he realized the value of newspaper clippings very early in his writing career. Twenty-five years ago he began to scissor and to put away those clippings which most impressed him. Until late in the year 1893 his clipping collection was either pasted in scrap-books or thrown loosely into a large box. During the winter of 1893—4 he felt the necessity of having the raw material of his Factory stored more systematically. The services of an assistant were secured and the work was begun.

Large manila envelopes were used. The envelopes were lettered alphabetically, and each clipping was filed by title. On the back of each envelope was typed the title of its contents.

This method was found to be wholly unsatisfactory. Frequent examination had given Edwards a fair working knowledge of his thousands of clippings, but he was often obliged to go through a dozen or more envelopes before finding the particular article whose title had escaped him.

In 1905 he bought a loose-leaf book and tried out a new system on an accumulation of several thousand magazines. This indexing was done in such a way as to suggest the character of the clipping (written in red), and the title of the article, the page number and number of the magazine (written in black). All the magazines had been numbered consecutively and placed on convenient shelves. The first page of "W," for instance, appeared as shown below:

Washington "A Job in the Senate" 771-3
Wild Animal Story "The Rebellion of a Millionaire" 477-4
Washington, Booker T. "Riddle of the Negro" 519-4
White Cross "Work of the American W. C." 129-5
Waitress "Diary of an Amateur W." 543-6
Wall Street "The Shadow of High Finance" 336-8
Woman Suffrage "Worlds Half-Citizens" 411-8
Woman "How to Make Money" 495-9

The above is only part of one of many pages of W's, and will serve to exemplify the advantages and disadvantages of the system in practical use. For instance, if it was desired to find out something about Booker T. Washington, all that was necessary was to take down old magazine No. 4 and turn to page 519.

This manifestly was an improvement over the old envelope method of indexing, but still left much to be desired. To illustrate, if Edwards wished to exhaust his material on Booker T. Washington it was necessary for him to hunt through all the pages under "W," and then examine all the magazines containing the articles in which he was mentioned. It is patent that if the indexing were properly done, every reference having to do with Booker T. Washington should follow a single reference to him in the index; and, further, the various articles should be grouped together.

Two years later, Edwards discarded the loose-leaf for the card system. This, he found, was as near perfection as could be hoped for.

His first step was to buy a number of strong box letter-files. These he numbered consecutively, just as he had numbered the manila envelopes. Articles are cut from magazines, the leaves secured together with brass fasteners, and on the first page margin at the top are marked the file number and letter of compartment where the article belongs. Thus, if the article is kept out of the file for any length of time it can be readily returned to its proper place. Newspaper clippings are handled in precisely the same way.

The card index has its divisions and sub-divisions. Cards indexing articles on various countries have a place under the general letter, and another place in the geographical section under the same letter. So with articles concerning Noted Personages, Astronomy, Antiquities, etc. Below, for the benefit of any one who may wish to use the system, is reproduced a card from the file:

ARMY, U. S.

Hand Bill used to secure enlistments	"A"	1
Army Story "Knew It"	"K"	1
Army Story "A Philippine Romance"	"P"	1
Army Story "He is Crazy Jack"	"C"	1
Army Story "Their Very Costly Meal"	"T"	1
Army Story "Siege of Bigbag"	"S"	1
"Fighting Life in the Phillippines"	"F"	1
Pay of Soldiers "Young Man—"	"Y"	2

In this system the character of the material is first indicated, as *Pay of Soldiers*. If there is a title it follows in quotation marks. Where the title suggests the character of the material sufficiently, the title comes first, in "quotes." Then follows the letter under which the article is filed, and the number of the file. Suppose it is desired to find out what soldiers of the United States' Army are paid for their services: File No. 2 is removed from the shelf, opened at letter "Y" and the information secured under title beginning, "Young Man —."

As a saver of time, and a guard against annoyance when fancies are running free, Edwards has found his card-index system for clippings almost ideal.

A friend of Edwards' is what the comic papers call a "jokesmith." Recently he concocted the following:

"You must be doing well," said Jones the merchant to Quill the writer, meeting him in front of his house. "You seem to be always busy, and you look prosperous."

"So I am, Jones," answered Quill, "busy and prosperous. Come into the basement with me and I'll show you the secret of my prosperity."

They decended into the basement and Quill rang up the curtain on a ragman weighing three big bags of rejection slips.

"My stories all come back," confessed Quill, triumphantly, "and I get three cents a pound for the rejection slips that come with them."

This, of course, was not much of a joke, but the prepetrator sent it to *Judge*. *Judge* sent it back with about twenty blank rejection slips inclosed by a rubber band. On the top slip was written: "Here are some more.—Ed. *Judge*."

X.

THE WOLF
AT THE DOOR

Perhaps very few men in this life escape a period as black and dispiriting as was the year 1897 for Edwards. If not in one way, then in another, it is the fate of a man to be chastened and subdued so thoroughly, at least once in his career, that a livid rememberance of it remains always with him. Edwards has always been an optimist, but those blows of circumstance of the year 1897 found many weak places in the armor of his philosophy.

In tangling and untangling the threads of a story plot Edwards had become tolerably proficient, but in straightening out the snarls Fate had made in his own life he was crushed with a feeling of abject helplessness. There is a vast difference, it seems, in dealing with the complications of others and those that beset ourselves. The impersonal attitude makes for keener analysis and wiser judgment.

In a story, the poverty stricken hero and his wife may exist for a week on a loaf of bread, ten cents' worth of potatoes and a twenty-cent soup-bone; but let the man who creates such a hero attempt to emulate his fictional fancies and stark realism plays havoc with the equation. The wolf at our own door is one sort of animal, and the wolf at our neighbor's is of an altogether different breed.

THE FICTION FACTORY

The thermometer in Southern Arizona was "eighty in the shade" when Mr. and Mrs. Edwards, during the Christmas holidays, set their faces eastward. New York City, the shrine of so many pilgrims seeking prosperity, was their goal; and the metropolis, on that bleak New Year's Day that witnessed their arrival, was shivering in the grip of real, old-fashioned winter. The change from a balmy climate to blizzards and ice and a below-zero temperature brought Edwards to his bed with a vicious attack of rheumatism. For day's while the little fund of $100 melted steadily away, he lay helpless.

The great city, in its dealings with impecunious strangers, has been painted in cruel colors. Edwards found this to be a mistake. On the occasion of their first visit to New York he and his wife had found quarters in a boarding house in Forty-fourth street. A pleasant landlady was in charge and the Edwards had won her friendship.

Here, forming one happy family, were actors and actresses, a salesman in a down-town department store, a stenographer, a travelling man for a bicycle house, and others. All were cheerful and kindly, and took occasion to drop in at the Edwards' third floor front and beguile the tedious hours for the invalid.

Fourteen years have brought many changes to Forty-fourth street between Broadway and Sixth avenue. The row of high-stoop brownstone "fronts" has that air of neglect which precedes demolition and the giving way of the old order to the new. The basement, where the pleasant landlady sat at her long table and smiled at the raillery and wit of "Beaney," and Sam, and "Smithy," and Ruth, and Ina and the rest, has fallen sadly from its high estate. A laundry has taken possession of the place. And "Beaney," the light-hearted one who laughed at his own misfortunes and sympathized with the misfortunes of others, "Beaney" has gone to his long account. A veil as impenetrable has fallen over the pleasant landlady, Sam, "Smithy," Ruth and Ina; and wherever they may be, Edwards, remembering their kindness to him in his darkest days, murmurs for each and all of them a fervent "God bless you!" . . . . . .

Before he was compelled to take to his bed Edwards had called at the offices of Harte & Perkins. His interview with Mr. Perkins impressed upon him the fact that, once a place upon the contributors' staff of a big publishing house is relinquished it is difficult to regain. Others had been given the work which Edwards had had for three years. These others were turning in acceptable manuscripts and, in justice to them, Harte & Perkins could not take the work out of their hands. Mr. Perkins, however, did give Edwards an order for four Five-Cent Libraries—stories to be held in reserve in case manuscripts from regular contributors failed to arrive in time. On Feb. 11 he received a letter from the firm to the following effect:

"When we wrote you day before yesterday asking you to turn in four Five-Cent Libraries before doing anything else in the Library line for us, we were under the impression that the gentleman who has been engaged upon this work for some time would not be able to turn the material in with usual regularity on account of illness, but we hear from him today that he is now in better health, and will be able to keep up with the work, which he is very anxious to do, and somewhat jealous of having any other material in the series so long as he can fill the bill. On this account it will be well for you to stop work on the

Library. When you have completed the story on which you are now engaged, turn your attention to the Ten-Cent Library work, which we think you will be able to do to our satisfaction."

This will illustrate the attitude which some authors assume toward the "butter-in." All of a certain grist that comes to a publisher's mill must be *their* grist. If the mill ground for another, and found the product better than ordinary, the other might secure a "stand-in" that would threaten the prestige of the regular contributor.

In seeking to keep his head above water financially, Edwards attempted to sell book rights of "The Astrologer," the serial published in 1891 in *The Detroit Free Press.* He had written, also, 66 pages of a present-tense Gunteresque story which he hoped would win favor as had his other stories in that style. This yarn he called "Croesus, Jr." Both manuscripts were submitted to Harte & Perkins.

On Jan. 28, when the Edwards' exchequer was nearly depleted, "Croesus, Jr.," was returned with this written message:

"It might be said of the story in a way that it is readable, but it does not promise as good a story as we desire for this series. 'Most decidedly,' says the reader, 'it lacks originality, novelty and strength.' This criticism, which we consider entirely competent, must deter us from considering the story favorably."

This was blow number one. Blow number two was delivered Feb. 3:

"We have had your manuscript, 'The Astrologer,' examined, and the verdict is that it would not be suitable for any of our regular publications, and it is not in our line for book publication. The reader states that it very humorous in parts but rather long drawn out........We return manuscript."

Two Five-Cent Libraries at $40 each were accepted and paid for; also four sketches written for a small magazine which Harte & Perkins were starting.*

Although he grew better of his rheumatism, Edwards failed to improve materially in health, and late in March he and his wife returned to Chicago. They rented a modest flat on the North Side, got their household effects out of storage, and faced the problem of existence with a courage scarcely warranted by their circumstances.

Edwards was able to work only half a day. The remainder of the day he spent in bed with an alternation of chills and fever and a grevious malady growing upon him. During this period he tried syndicating articles in the newspapers but without success. He also wrote for Harte & Perkins a *"Guest"* serial, the order for which he had brought back with him from New York. He made one try for this by submitting the first few chapters and synopsis of story which he called "A Vassar Girl." These were returned to him as unsuitable. He then wrote seven chapters of a serial entitled, "A Girl from the Backwoods," and—with much fear and trembling be it confessed—sent them on for examination. Under date of July 8 this word was deturned:

"The seven chapters of 'A Girl from the Backwoods' read very good, and we should like to have you finish the story, and should it prove satisfactory in its entirely, we should consider it an acceptable story."

Here was encouragement at a time when encouragement was sorely needed. But how to keep the Factory

*This magazine, by the way, which had an humble beginning, has grown into one of the high class "populars" and has a wide circulation.

going while the story was being finished was a difficult question. There were times when twenty-five cents had to procure a Sunday dinner for two; and there was a time when two country cousins arrived for a visit, and Edwards had not the half-dollar to pay an expressman for bringing their trunks from the station! Pride, be it understood, was one of Edwards' chief assets. He had always been a regal spender, and his country cousins knew it. How the lack of that fifty-cent piece grilled his sensitive soul!

It was during these trying times that the genius of Mrs. Edwards showed like a star in the heavy gloom. On next to nothing she contrived to supply the table, and the conjuring she could do with a silver dollar was a source of never-failing wonder to her husband.

Edwards remembers that, at a time when there was not even car-fare in the family treasury, a check for $1.50 arrived in payment for a 1,500-word story that had been out for several years.

During the latter part of July the demand for money pending the completion of "A Girl from the Backwoods" became so insistent, that Edwards wrote and submitted to Harte & Perkins a sketch for their magazine. It contained 1,232 words and was purchased on Aug. 3 for $6.16.

"A Girl from the Backwoods" was submitted late in September, and was returned on Oct. 13 for a small correction. The following letter, dated Oct. 27, was received from the editor of the "Guest:"

"The manuscript of 'A Girl from the Backwoods', also the correction which you have made, have been duly received. The correction is very satisfactory.

In regard to your suggestion about the heroine's name being that of a well known writer, we would say that inasmuch as the name is rather appropriate and suits the character we do not see that the lady who already bears it would in any way find fault with your use of it, and at present we think it may be allowed to stand."

As showing Edwards' pecuniary distress, the following paragraph from a letter from Harte & Perkins, dated Oct. 28, may be given:

"In response to your favor of the 19th and your telegram of yesterday, * we enclose you herewith our check for $200 in full for your story 'A Girl from the Backwoods.' This is the best price we can make you for this and other stories of this class from your pen, and it is a somewhat better one than we are now paying for similar material from other writers. We believe this will be satisfactory to you."

The price was not saticfactory. Edwards and his wife had counted upon receiving at least $300 for the story, and they needed that amount sorely. A respectful letter at once went forward to Harte & Perkins, appealing to their sense of justice and fairness, which Edwards had never yet known to fail him. On Nov. 3 came an additional check for $100, and these words:

"Replying to your favor of Nov. 1st, at hand today, we beg to state that we shall, agreeably with your request and especially as you put it in such strong terms, make the payment on 'A Girl from the Backwoods' $300. The story is much liked by our reader and we do think it is worth as much if not more than the Stella Edwards material which, however, in the writer's judgement was much overpaid. We shall take this into account when considering the acceptance of other stories from your pen, and while we do not say positively that we will not pay $300 for the next one, as we wrote you in our last letter this is a high price for this class of material and we will expect to pay you according to our views as to the value of the manuscript."

The year closed with an order from Harte & Perkins for another story of the Stella Edwards sort; a

*Telegram sent on same day letter was received saying story was satisfactory.

very dismal year indeed, and showing Factory returns as
follows:

Two Five-Cent Libraries at $40	$ 80.00
Four magazine sketches at $10	40.00
One magazine sketch	6.16
"A Girl from the Backwoods,"	300.
Total	$426.16

Perhaps, after all, this was not doing so badly; for
during this year, and the year immediately following,
Edwards was to discover that he had had one foot in the
grave. But his fortunes were at their lowest ebb. With
1898 they were to begin taking an upward turn.

Some one said that some one else, by using Ignatius
Donnelly's cryptogram, proved that the late Bill Nye
wrote the Shakespeare plays. This, of course, is merely
a reflection on the cryptogram; BUT if Shakespeare's
publishers had not been so slovenly with that folio edition of his plays, there would never have been any
hunt for a cipher, nor any of this Bacon talk.

———

"In the early days, when I lived on the plains of
Western Kansas on a homestead," says John H. Whit-
son, well and favorably known to dozens of editors, "I
was nosed out by a correspondent for a Kansas City
paper, who thought there was something bizarre in the
fact that an author was living the simple life of a Western Settler. The purported interview he published was
wonderful concoction! He gave a descriptive picture of
the dug-out in which I lived, and filled in the gaps with
other matter drawn from his imagination, making me
out a sort of literary troglodyte; whereas, as a matter
of fact, I had never lived in a dug-out. On top of it, one
of my homesteading friends asked me in all seriousness
how much I had paid to get that write-up and picture in
the Kansas City paper, and seemed to think I was doing
some tall lying when I said I had paid nothing."

XI

WHEN FICTION IS
STRANGER THAN TRUTH.

We are told that "fiction hath in it a higher end than fact," which we may readily believe; and we may also concede that "truth is stranger than fiction," at least in its occasional application. Nevertheless, in the course of his career as a writer Edwards has created two fictional fancies which so closely approximated truth as to make fiction stranger than truth; and, in one case, the net result of imagination was to coincide exactly with real facts of which the imagination could take no account. Perhaps each of these two instances is unique in its particular field; they are, in any event, so odd as to be worthy of note.

In the early 90's, when a great deal of Edwards' work was appearing, unsigned, in *The Detroit Free Press,* he wrote for that paper a brief sketch entitled, "The Fatal Hand." The sketch was substantially as follows:

"The Northern Pacific Railroad had just been built into Helena, Montana, and I happened to be in the town one evening and stepped into a gambling hall. Burton, a friend of mine, was playing poker with a miner and two professional gamblers. I stopped beside the table and watched the game.

Cards had just been drawn. Burton, as soon as he had looked at his hand, calmly shoved the cards together, laid them face-downward in front of him, removed a notebook from his pocket and scribbled something on a blank leaf. 'Read that,' said he, 'when you get back to your hotel tonight.'

The play proceeded Presently the miner detected one of the professional gamblers in the act of cheating. Words were passed, the lie given. All the players leaped to their feet. Burton, in attempting to keep the miner from shooting, received the gambler's bullet and fell dead upon the scattered cards.

An hour later, when I reached my hotel, I thought of the note Burton had handed me. It read: 'I have drawn two red sevens. I now hold jacks full on red sevens. It is a fatal hand and I shall never leave this table alive. I have $6,000 in the First National Bank at Bismarck. Notify my mother, Mrs. Ezra J. Burton, Louisville, Kentucky.' "

This small product of the Fiction Factory was pure fiction from beginning to end. In the original it had the tang of point and counterpoint which caused it to be seized upon by other papers and widely copied. This gave extensive publicity to the "fatal hand"—the three jacks and two red sevens contrived by Edwards out of a small knowledge of poker and the cabala of cards.

Yet, what was the result?

A month later the Chicago papers published an account of a police raid on a gambling room. As the officers rushed into the place a man at one of the tables fell forward and breathed his last. "Heart disease," was the verdict. But note: A police officer looked at the cards the dead man had held and found them to be *three jacks and two red sevens.*

A week later *The New York Recorder* gave space to a news story in which a man was slain at a gaming table in Texas. When the smoke of the shooting had blown away some one made the discovery that he had held the fatal hand.

From that time on for several months the fatal hand left a trail of superstition and gore all over the West. How many murders and hopeless attacks of heart failure it was responisble for Edwards had no means of knowing, but he could scarcely pick up a paper without finding an account of some of the ravages caused by his "jacks full on red sevens."

Query: Were the reporters of the country romancing? If not, will some psychologist kindly rise and explain how a bit of fiction could be responsible for so much real tragedy?

In this instance, fancy established a precedent for fact; in the case that follows, the frankly fictitious paralleled the unknown truth in terms so exact that the story was recognized and appropriated by the son of the story's hero.

While Edwards was in Arizona he was continually on the alert for story material. The sun, sand and solitude of the country "God forgot" produce types to be found nowhere else. He ran out many a trail that led from adobe-walled towns into waterless deserts and bleak, cacti-covered hills to end finally at some mine or cattle camp. It was on one of these excursions that he was told how a company of men had built a dam at a place called Walnut Grove. This dam backed up the waters of a river and formed a huge lake. Mining for gold by the hydraulic method was carried on profitably in the river below the dam. One night the dam "went out" and a number of laborers were drowned.

With this as the germ of the plot Edwards worked out a story. He called it "A Study in Red," and it purported to show how a lazy Maricopa Indian, loping along on his pony in the gulch below Walnut Grove, gave up his mount to a white girl, daughter of the superintendent of the mining company, and while she raced on to safety he remained to die in the flood from the broken dam.

THE FICTION FACTORY

The story was published in *Munsey's Magazine*. *Six years later* the author received a letter from the Maricopa Indian Reservation, sent to New York in care of the F. A. Munsey Company. The letter was from a young Maricopa.

"I have often read the account of my father's bravery, and how he saved the life of the beautiful white girl when the Walnut Grove dam gave way. I have kept the magazine, and whenever I feel blue, or life does not go to please me, I get the story and read it and take heart to make the best of my lot and try to pattern after my father.

I have long wanted to write you, and now I have done so. I am back from the Indian School at Carlisle, on a visit to my people, and am impelled to send you this letter of appreciation and thanks for the story about my father."

Now, pray, what is one to think of this? The letter bears all the earmarks of a *bona fide* performance and was written and mailed on the Reservation. Edwards' fiction, it seems, had become sober fact for this young Maricopa Indian. Or did his father really die by giving up his pony to the "beautiful young white girl?" And was Edwards' prescience doing subliminal stunts when he wrote the story?

John Peter, should this ever meet your eyes will you please communicate further with the author of "A Study in Red?" It has been some years now since a letter, sent to you at the Reservation, failed of a reply. And the letter has not been returned.

XII

FORTUNE BEGINS
TO SMILE

Edwards' literary fortunes all but reached financial zero in 1897; with 1898 they began to mount, although the tendency upward was not very pronounced until the month of April. During the first quarter of the year he wrote and sold one Stella Edwards serial entitled "Lovers En Masque." His poor health continued, and he was able to work only a few hours each day, but the fact that he could drive himself to the typewriter and lash his wits into evolving acceptable work gave him encouragement to keep at it. Early in April, with part of the proceeds from the serial story for expenses, he made a trip to New York.

"Prospecting trips" is the name Edwards gives to his frequent journeys to the publishing center of the country. He prospected for orders, prospected for better prices, prospected for new markets. No fiction factory can be run successfully on a haphazard system for disposing of its product. There must be some market in prospect, and on the wheel of this demand the output must be shaped as the potter shapes his clay.

Edwards made it a rule to meet his publishers once a year, secure their personal views as he could not secure them through correspondence, and keep himself prominently before them. In this way he secured commissions which, undoubtedly, would otherwise have been placed elsewhere. With each succeeding journey Edwards has made to New York, his prospecting trips have profited him more and more. This is as it should be. There is no "marking time" for a writer in the fierce competition for editorial favor; for one merely to "hold his own" is equivalent to losing ground. The writer must *grow* in his work. When he ceases to do that he will find himself slipping steadily backward toward oblivion.

Edwards found that in reaching New York in early April 1898, he had arrived at the psychological moment. Harte & Perkins, already described as keeping tense fingers on the pulse of their reading public, had discovered a feverish quickening of interest for which the Klondike gold rush was responsible. The prognosis was good for a new five-cent library; so the "Golden Star Library" was given to the presses. Edwards, because he was on the spot and urging his claims for recognition, was chosen to furnish the copy. During the year he wrote sixteen of these stories.

For half of April and all of May and June, Edwards and his wife were at their old boarding place in Forty-fourth street. During this time, along with the writing of the Golden Star stories, a juvenile serial and a Stella Edwards serial were prepared. The title of the Stella Edwards rhapsody was "A Blighted Heart."

On July 2, owing to the excessive heat in the city and a belief on Edwards' part that the country would benefit him, the Fiction Factory was temporarily removed to the Catskill Mountains. Comfortable quarters were secured in a hotel near Cairo, and the work of producing copy went faithfully on. Edwards' health improved somewhat, although he was still unable to keep at his machine for a union day of eight hours.

Under date of Aug. 1, Harte & Perkins wrote Edwards that on account of the poor success of the Golden Star Library they would have to stop its weekly publication and issue it as a monthly. Mr. Perkins write:

"I do not think that the quality of the manusccript is so much at fault as the character of the library itself, though it is very difficult always to know just what the boys want."

Edwards was depending upon this library to support himself and wife, and the weekly check was a *sine qua non*. Summer-resorting is expensive, and he had not yet had his fill of the historic old Catskills. He wrote the firm and requested them to send on a check for "A Blighted Heart." The blight did not confine itself to the story but was visited upon Edwards' hopes, as well. Harte & Perkins did not respond favorably. The serial was not to begin in *"The Weekly Guest"* until the latter part of September, and upon beginning publication was to be paid for in weekly installments of $25. Wrote Mr. Perkins:

"This is a season when, with depressed business and the many accounts we have to look after, it is difficult for us to make advanced payments on manuscripts. You may rest assured that, if conditions were otherwise, I should have been glad to meet your wishes."

This meant an immediate farewell to the stamping grounds of good old Rip Van Winkle. Forthwith the Edwards struck their tent and boarded a night boat at Catskill Landing for down river. In their stateroom that night, with a fountain pen and using the washstand for a table, Edwards completed No. 16 of the ill-fated Golden Star Library. He had begun this manuscript before the notification to stop work on the series had reached him. In such cases, Harte & Perkins never refused to accept the complete story.

December found Edwards again settled on the North Side, in Chicago. He had consulted a physician regarding his health, and after a thorough examination had been told that it would require at least a year, and perhaps a year and a half, to cure him. The physician was a young man of splendid ability, and as he had just "put out his shingle" and patients were slow in rallying "round the standard," he threw himself heart and soul into the task of making a whole man out of Edwards. The writer helped by leasing a flat within half a block of his medical adviser and faced the twelve or eighteen months to come with more or less equanimity.

Edwards, of course, could not recline at his ease while the work of rehabilitation was going forward. The family must be supported and the doctor paid. Forty dollars a month from the Golden Star Library would not do this. It was necessary to run up the returns somehow and another Stella Edwards story was undertaken. The title of this story was "Won by Love," and Harte & Perkins acknowledged receipt of the first two installemnts on Dec. 6. Inasmuch as "Won by Love" came very near being the death of its author, it may be interesting to consider the story a little further. The letter of the 6th ran:

"We have received the first two installments of 'Won by Love' and like them very much indeed, but before giving you a definite answer we would like to have four more instalments on approval, making six in all. Kindly send these at your earliest convenience and oblige."

The four installments were sent and nothing more was heard from them until a telegram, dated Jan. 19, 1899, was received:

"Please send more of 'Won by Love' as soon as possible. Must have it Monday."

Owing to the fact that the writer of the old Five-Cent Library, for which Edwards had furnished copy some years before, had been taken seriously ill, this work had been turned over to Edwards on Dec. 27, 1898.

At this time Edwards was confined to his bed, and there he worked, his typewriter in front of him on an improvised table. He had just finished several hours' work on a library story when the telegram regarding "Won by Love" was received. This was Saturday. Edwards wired at once that he would send two more installments on the following Monday. These 12,000 words went forward according to schedule, and on the night they were sent the doctor called and found his patient in a state of collapse. Cause, too much "Won by Love." The young physician took it more to heart than Edwards did.

"I'm afraid," said he gloomily, "that you have ended your writing for all time."

"You're wrong, doctor," declared Edwards; "I'm not going to be removed until I've done something better than pot-boilers."

"I want to call a specialist into consultation," was the reply.

The specialist was called and Edwards was stripped and his body marked off into sections—mapped out with one medical eye on the "undiscovered country" and the other on this lowly but altogether lovely "vale of tears." When the examination was finished, the preponderance of testimony was all in favor of the Promised Land.

"I should say, Mr. Edwards," said the specialist, in a tone professionally sympathetic, "that you have one chance in three to get well. Your other chance is for possibly seven or eight years of life. The third chance allows you barely time to settle your affairs."

Settle his affairs! What affairs had Edwards to settle? There was the next library to be written and "Won by Love" to finish, but these would have netted Mrs. Edwards no more than $340. And the smallest chance would not suffer Edwards to leave his wife even this pittance. Since his disastrous Arizona experience Edwards had not been able to save any money. He was only just beginning to look ahead to a little garnering when the doctors pronounced their verdict. He had not a dollar of property, real or personal, if his library was not taken into account, and not a cent of life insurance. After turning this deplorable situation over in his mind, he decided that it was impossible for him to die.

"I'm going to take the first chance," said he, "and make the most of it."

He did. The young physician gave up more of his time and worked like a galley slave to see his patient through. Now, thirteen years after the specialist spoke the last word, Edwards is in robust health—the monument of his own determination and the young doctor's skill. Nothing succeeds—sometimes—like the logic of *nil desperandum*.

To regain a foothold with his publishers, following the disastrous year of 1897, had cost Edwards so much persistent work that he would not cancel a single order. He hired a stenographer and for two weeks dictated his stories, then again resumed the writing of them himself, in bed and with the use of the improvised table. Success awaited all his fiction, even when turned out in such adverse circumstances. This, perhaps, was the best tonic he could have. He improved slowly but surely and was able, in addition to his regular work, to write a hundred-thousand word novel embracing his Arizona experiences. This novel he called "He Was a Stranger."

The title was awkward, but it had been clipped from the quotation, "he was a stranger, and they took him in." The story was submitted to Harte & Perkins, but they were not in the mood for taking in strangers of that sort. But the year following the novel secured the friendly consideration of Mr. Matthew White, Jr., and introduced Edwards into the Munsey publications.

Another novel, " The Man from Dakota," was returned by Harte & Perkins after they had had it on hand for a year. It was declined in the face of a favorable report by one of their readers because, "We have so many books on hand that must be brought out during the next year that we cannot consider this story."

The year 1899 closed with Fortune's smile brightening delightfully for Edwards, and the new century beckoning him pleasantly onward with the hope of better things to come. The returns for the two years, standing to the credit of The Fiction Factory, are summarized thus:

1898:
"Lovers En Masque,".......................$ 300.
"Golden Star Library," 16 at $40 each,...... 640.

```
Boys Serial, ............................. .............   100.
"A Blighted Heart," .......................   300.

            Total ................. $1340.
1899:
"Won by Love," ........................... $ 300.
3 "Golden Stars" at $40 each, ...............   120.
35 Five-Cent Libraries at $40 each, .......... 1400.

            Total ................. $1820.
```

Edwards lives in the outskirts of a small town, on a road much travelled by farmers. Two honest tillers of the soil were passing his home, one day, and one of them was heard to remark to the other: "A man by the name of Edwards lives there, Jake. He's one of those fictitious writers."

Edwards has few friends whom he prizes more highly than he does Col. W. F. Cody, "Buffalo Bill," and Major Gordon W. Lillie, "Pawnee Bill." While the Wild West and Far East Show, of which Cody and Lillie are the proprietors was making its farewell tour with the Last of the Scouts, Major Lillie had this to tell about Colonel Cody:

"You'd be surprised at the number of people who try to beat their way into the show by stringing the Colonel. The favorite way is by claiming acquaintance with him. A stranger will approach Buffalo Bill with a bland smile and an outstretched hand. 'Hello, Colonel!' he'll say, 'guess who I am! I'll bet you can't guess who I am!' Cody will give it up. 'Why,' bubbles the stranger, 'don't you remember when you were in Ogden, Utah, in nineteen-two? Remember the crowd at the depot to see you get off the train? Why, I was the man in the white hat!'"

"Just this afternoon," laughed the Major, "Cody came up to where I was standing. He was wiping the sweat from his forehead and his face was red and full of disgust. 'What's the matter?' I inquired. 'Oh,' he answered, 'another one of those d— guessing contests! Why in blazes can't people think up something new?'"

XIII.

OUR FRIEND,
THE T. W.

In some localities of this progressive country the pen
may still be mightier than the sword; but if, afar from
railroad and telegraph, holed away in barbaric seclusion,
there really exists a community that writes with a quill
and uses elderberry ink and a sandbox, it is safe to say
that this community has never been heard of—and the
cause is not far to seek. Just possibly, however, it is
from such a backwoods township that the busy editor
receives those rare manuscripts whose chirography covers both sides of the sheet. In this case the pen is
really mightier than the sword as an instrument for cut-
ting the ground out from under the feet of aspiring genius. Just possibly, too, it was from such a place that a
typewritten letter was returned to the sender with the
indignant scrawl: "You needn't bother to print my letters—I can read writin'."

Nowadays penwork is confined largely to signing
letters and other documents and indorsing checks; to
use it for anything else should be named a misdemeanor
in the statutes with a sliding scale of punishments to fit
the gravity of the offense.

It is not to be inferred, of course, that a man will dictate his love letters to a stenographer. Here, indeed,
"two's company and three's a crowd." Every man
should master the T. W., and when he confides his tender
sentiments to paper for the eyes of the One Girl, his

own fingers should manipulate the keys and the T. W., should be equipped with a tri-chrome ribbon—red and black record and purple copying. Black will answer for the more subdued expressions, red should be switched on for the warmer terms of endearment, and purple should be used for whatever might be construed as evidence in a court of law. Even *billets-doux* have been known to develop a commercial value.

When a serviceable typewriter may be bought for $25 what excuse has anyone for side-stepping the inventive ingenuity of the day which makes for clearness and speed? How much does Progress owe the typewriter? Who can measure the debt? How much does civilization owe the telephone, the night-letter, the fast mail and two-cent postage? Even more than to these does Progress owe to that mechanism of springs, keys and type-bars which makes plain and rapid the written thought.

In the Edwards Fiction Factory the T. W., comprises the entire "plant." The "hands" employed for the skilled labor are his own, and fairly proficient. His own, too, is the administrative ability, modest enough in all truth yet able to guide the Factory's destiny with a fair meed of success.

Since the T. W., is so important, Edwards believes in always keeping abreast of improvements. The best is none too good. A typed script, no less than a stereotyped idea, is damned by mediocrity. If a typewriter appears this year which is a distinct advance over last year's machine, Edwards has it. Keeping up-to-date is usually a little expensive, but it pays.

In the early days of his writing Edwards used the old Caligraph. It was a small machine and confined itself to capital letters. Whenever he wished to indicate the proper place for a capital he did it thus: HIS NAME WAS CAESAR, AND HE LIVED IN ROME. If he lost a letter—and letters in those days were not easily replaced—he allowed the unknown quantity "X" to piece out: HIX NAME WAX CAEXAR—. In due time he came to realize the importance of neatness and traded his first Caligraph for a later model equipped with letters from both "cases." During twenty-two years he has purchased at least twenty-five typewriters, each the last word in typewriter construction at the time it was bought. At present he has two machines, one a "shift-key" and the other with every letter and character separately represented on the key-board.

There are many makes of typewriters, and operators are of many minds regarding the "best" makes. Edwards has favored the full key-board as being less of a drain upon the attention than the "shift-key" machine. For the writer who composes upon his machine the operating must become a habit, otherwise an elusive idea may take wings for good while the one who evolved it is searching out the letters necessary to nail it hard and fast to the white sheet. Edwards has recently discovered that he can change from his full key-board to a shift-key and back again without materially interrupting his flow of ideas.

The characters of the key-board used for ordinary business purposes and those in demand by the writer are somewhat different. Not always, on the key-board designed for commercial use, will the exclamation point be found. This, if wanted, must be built up out of a period and a half-ditto mark,—"." plus " ' " equals "!" Such makeshifts should be tabooed by the careful writer. Whatever is worth doing at all is worth doing well, and *once*. Three motions, two at the key-board and one at the back-spacer, are two too many. By all means have the real thing in exclamation points—!

Another makeshift with which Edwards has little patience is the custom of using ditto marks for quotation marks, and semi-dittos for semi-quotes. These, and other characters, may be added to most machines by eliminating the fractions, the oblique mark or the per cent. sign.

Is seems poor policy, also, to use a hyphen, or two hyphens, to indicate a dash. Why not have the under-score raised to the position of a hyphen and so have a dash that *is* a dash?

The asterisk, "*," is a character valuable for indicating footnotes , and the caret is often useful in making typewritten interlineations. All these characters Edwards has on his full key-board machine. On the shift-key machine he must still struggle with the built-up exclamation point, the ditto quotes and the hyphen dash. No wonder he prefers a Smith Premier!

Even the best and most up-to-date typewriter cannot answer all the demands made upon it by writers, however. Some day the growing army of authors will receive due attention in this matter, and the manuscript submitted to editors will compare favorably with the printed story.

THE FICTION FACTORY

In "Habits that Help," a very instructive article by
Walter D. Scott, professor of psychology at Northwest-
ern University, published in *Everybody's Magazine* for
September, 1911, appears this paragraph:

"Some time ago I could pick out the lettters on a typewriter at
a rate of about one per second. Writing is now becoming
reduced to a habit, and I can write perhaps three letters a second.
When the act has been reduced to the pure habit form, I shall be
writing at the rate of not less than five letters per second."

The "pure habit form" is one for those who compose
on the typewriter to acquire. It not only means ease of
composition, but speed in the performance and perfect
legibility.

Until a few years ago, Edwards always carried his
typewriter with him on his travels. The machine was
large and heavy and had to be handled with care, so its
transportation was no easy matter. In course of time,
and pending the invention of a practical typewriter to fit
the pocket, he became content to leave his machine at
home and rent one wherever he happened to be.

During one of his eastern "prospecting" trips, Edwards and his wife left New York for a few summer
weeks in the Berkshire Hills. The T. W., remained
temporarily in the city to be overhauled and forwarded.
For a fortnight Edwards slaved with a pen, *writing four
manuscripts of 25,000 words each.* He appreciated then,
as he had never done before, the value of the typewriter
in his work. Late in the first week he began writing
and telegraphing for his machine to be sent on.

About the hotel it was known that Edwards expected
a typewriter by every stage from Great Barrington. He
had fretted about the non-arrival of the typewriter, and
in some manner had let fall the information that his

typewriter weighed sixty pounds. Speculation was rife as to whether the T. W., had blue eyes or gray, and as to what manner of dwarf or living skeleton could fulfill the requirements at sixty pounds. When the machine finally arrived and the square packing case was unloaded, a host of curious ladies received the surprise of their lives.

"Typewriter," commonly used as a generic name for the machine that prints, as well as for the person who operates it, should have its double meaning curtailed. The young lady of pleasing face and amiable deportment, whose deft fingers hover over the keys of a senseless machine, is entitled to something more appropriate in the way of a professional title.

Let it be "typist," after the English fashion; and instead of saying "the typist typewrote the letter," why not say she "typed" it?

An editor once returned a manuscript with a note like this:

Dear Sir:—Put it into narrative form.
Yours truly, "The Editor."

I did so. A week later came this:

"Dear Sir :—A little mystery would help. We like your style very much. Yours truly, "The Editor."

I put in the mystery. A week later,—

"Dear Sir:—You send us good verse. Why not turn the marked paragraphs into verse, with strong influence on story? Well written. "Yours truly, etc."

It was a good idea. The verse was acceptable. It was so acceptable that the editor sent back the story and a check for $5 in payment for the verse—which was all he kept!

XIV

FRESH FIELDS
AND PASTURES NEW

So far in his writing career Harte & Perkins had
been the heaviest purchasers of Edwards' fiction. They
had given him about all he could do of a certain class of
work, and he had not tried to find other markets for the
Factory's product. Pinning his hopes to one firm, even
though it was the best firm in the business, was unsatisfactory in many respects. For various reasons, any one
of which is good and sufficient, a writer should have
more than one "string to his bow." Harte & Perkins,
jealously watching the tastes of their reading public,
were compelled to make many and sudden changes in the
material they put out. This directly affected the writers
of the material, and Edwards was often left with no prospects at all, and perhaps at just the time when he flatter-
ed himself that his prospects were brightest.

In preceding chapters mention has been made of two
serial stories in which Edwards had vainly endeavored to
interest Harte & Perkins. One of these was "The Man
from Dakota," and the other, "He Was A Stranger."
These, and another entitled "A Tale of Two Towns,"
written late in 1900, were ultimately to open new markets.

In a diary for the year 1900, Edwards has this under
date of Tuesday, Jan. 2:

"Mr. Paisley called to see me this morning on a business matter. It appears that the proprietor of *The Western World* had ordered a serial from Opie Read and was not satisfied with it.* As *The Western World* goes to press in a few days they must have another story at once. Later in the day I talked with Mr. Underwood the (as I suppose) proprietor, and he asked me to get "The Man from Dakota" from Mr. Kerr, of *The Chicago Ledger*. I did so and took the manuscript over to Mr. Paisley. If it is acceptable they are to pay me $200 for it."

Mr. Paisley was a gentleman with whom Mrs. Edwards had become acquainted while attending Frank Holme's School for Illustration, in Chicago. He was a man of much ability.

Under Thursday, Jan. 4, the diary has a memorandum to this effect:

"Mr. Paisley came out to see me at noon. They like 'The Man from Dakota' and will pay me $200 for it, divided into three payments of $50, $50 and $100."

So, finally, "The Man from Dakota" got into print. While it was still appearing in *The Western World;* Mr. Underwood conceived the idea of booming the circulation of his paper by publishing a mystery story—one of those stories in which the mystery is not revealed until the last chapter, and for the solution of which prizes are offered. He asked Edwards if he would write such a story. Why should Edwards write one when he already had on hand the mystery story unsuccessfully entered in the old *Chicago Daily News* contest? He offered this to Mr. Underwood. He read it and liked it. Mr. Paisley read it and liked it. What was the very lowest figure Edwards would take for it?

Mr. Underwood, in getting around to this point, told how he had sent for Stanley Waterloo and asked him to

*What do you think of *that!*

write the mystery story. "What will you pay?" inquired Mr. Waterloo. "I'll give you $100," said Mr. Under-
wood. Whereupon Mr. Waterloo arose in awful majes-
ty and strode from the office. He did not even linger
to say good-by.

"Now," said Mr. Underwood to Edwards, with a
genial smile, "don't you do that if I offer you seventy-
five dollars for 'What Happened to the Colonel.' "

"Cash?" asked Edwards.

"On the nail."

"Give me the money," said Edwards; "I need it."

Now that the diary has been quoted with a reference
to Opie Read, perhaps another reference to the same
genial and talented gentleman may be pardoned:

Jan. 19, 1900.—"Opie Read made his 'first appearance in
vaudeville' this week, and Gertie (Mrs. Edwards) and I went
to the Chicago Opera House this afternoon to hear him. He
was very good, but I would rather read one of his stories than
hear him tell it."

Later in the year Edwards "broke into" the papers
served by the McClure Syndicate with "A Tale of Two
Towns." After using this serial in metropolitan papers,
the McClure people sold it to The Kellogg Newspaper
Union to be used in the "patents" sent out to country
newspapers. The story was later brought out in cloth
by the G. W. Dillingham Co., New York.

The third novel, "He Was A Stranger," had already
been refused by Harte & Perkins. Late in May, 1900,
Edwards again went "prospecting" to New York. Feeling positive that Harte & Perkins had missed some of the
good points in the story, he carried the manuscript with
him and once more submitted it. Again it was refused,
but Mr. Hall, editor of the "Guest," informed Edwards

that he had an excellent story but that it was impossible for Harte & Perkins to consider its purchase. Edwards asked if he knew of a possible market. "Mr. Munsey," was the reply, "is looking for stories for *The Argosy*, and I'd suggest that you take the story over there and show it to Mr. White, *The Argosy's* editor." Edwards tucked the novel under his arm and strolled up Fifth Avenue to the offices of the Frank A. Munsey Company. There, and for the first time, he met Mr. Matthew White, Jr.

The impression of power, tremendous ability and a big, two-handed grasp of *Argosy* affairs which the editor made upon Edwards, at this time, has deepened with the passing years. An author, as well as a keen dramatic critic, Mr. White brings to bear on his editorial duties an intuition that closely approximates genius. He has proved his remarkable fitness for the post he occupies by making *The Argosy*, since Mr. Munsey "divested it of its knickerbockers," the most widely read of all the purely fiction magazines. And withal he is one of the most pleasant editors whom a writer will ever have the good fortune to meet.

Mr. White was glad to consider "He Was A Stranger." He thumbed over the pages, noted the length, and asked what price Edwards would put upon the manuscript in case it was acceptable. Edwards named $500, and told of "The Brave and Fair" which Harte & Perkins, a few years before, had bought at that figure. Mr. White replied that *The Argosy*, as yet, was unable to pay such prices, but that he would read the story and, if he liked it, make an offer. A few days later he offered $250 for serial rights. Edwards took into consideration the fact that the story would establish him in the columns of a growing magazine and, with an eye to the future, accepted the offer. He has never had occasion to regret his decision.

From the beginning of the year Edwards had been doing a large amount of five-cent library work for Harte & Perkins. A new weekly had been started, the writer who furnished the copy failed to get his manuscript in on time, and Edwards was given a story to finish and, a few days afterward, the entire series to take care of.

At the time he sold the serial to Mr. White, he was supplying weekly copy for two libraries—the old Five-Cent Library and the new weekly, which shall here be referred to as the Circus Series.

On the proceeds from the sale of "He Was A Stranger" Edwards and his wife had a little outing at Atlantic City. They returned to New York for a few days, and then went on to Boston. Here, comfortably quartered in a hotel, Edwards devoted his mornings to work and his afternoons to seeing the "sights" with Mrs. Edwards. They haunted Old Cambridge, they made pilgrimages to Salem, to Plymouth and to other places, and they enjoyed themselves as they had never done before on an eastern trip. Later they finished out the summer near Monterey, in the Berkshire Hills.

During all these travels the Fiction Factory was regularly grinding out its grist of copy—so many pages a day, so many stories a week. Two libraries, together with a sketch each month for a trade paper published by Harte & Perkins, kept Edwards too busy to prepare any manuscripts for *The Argosy*. Much of his work, while

in the Berkshires, was done in longhand. On this point
Mr. Perkins wrote, July 25:

"I should think you would miss your typewriter. I fear that
I shall miss it, too, when I read your manuscript, although I
find your writing easier to read than that of any of our other
writers."

In August the Edwards went West, visited for a time
in Michigan and then in Wisconsin, finally returned to
the former state and, in the little country town where
Edwards was born, bought an old place and settled
down.

As with the Golden Star Library, misfortune finally
overtook the Circus Series. A telegram was received
telling Edwards to hold No. 47 of the Circus Series pending instructions by letter. The letter instructed him to
close up finally the adventures of the hero and his
friends and bring their various activities to an appropriate end. The series was continued, for a while longer, with a brand-new hero in each story; but Edwards
was requested to write but three of the stories in the new
form.

The year, which opened auspiciously and proved a
banner year financially, closed with a discontinuance of
all orders from Harte & Perkins. Re-prints were being
used in the old Five-Cent Library—stories that had been
issued years before and could now be republished for
another generation of boy readers. Under date of Dec.
1, 1911, Mr. Perkins wrote:

"I know of nothing, just at present, which you can do for
us, but should anything develop I shall be very glad to inform
you."

This left Edwards with a sketch a month for the
trade paper, for which he was paid $10 each. That

misfortunes never come singly'' is an old saying, and one which Edwards has found particularly true in the writing profession. A letter of Dec. 27, informed him:

"We have decided to dispense with the sketches in our trade paper for the present, at least; therefore the February sketch we have in hand will be the last we will want unless we give you further notice."

In a good many cases the tendency of a writer, when fate deals hardly with him in the matter of a demand for his work, is to take his rebuffs too seriously. Often he will lock up his Factory, leaving a placard on the door: "Closed. Proprietor gone to Halifax. Nothing in the fiction game anyhow.''

Edwards used to feel in this way. As he grew older he learned to take his disappointments with more or less equanimity, and to keep the Factory running. He thought, now, of Mr. White and *The Argosy*. Here was a good time to prepare an *Argosy* serial. He wrote it, sent it, and on Feb. 15, 1901, received this terse letter:

"My dear Mr. Edwards:
We can use your story, 'The Tangle in Butte,' in *The Argosy* at $200. Very truly yours,
Matthew White, Jr."

This was less than the price paid for "He Was A Stranger,'' but the story ran only 60,000 words, while the other serial had gone to 100,000. The acceptance went to Mr. White by return mail.

On the day following there came a letter from Harte & Perkins ordering work in the old Five-Cent Library—work that would keep Edwards busy for the rest of the year. Ten of the old stories which Edwards had written were to be revised and lengthened by 10,000 words. For this work he was to be paid $30 for each story. When the ten numbers had been revised and lengthened, he was to go on with the stories, writing a new one each week. Fifty dollars apiece was to be paid for the new stories.

There was an order, too, for more sketches for the trade paper, to be done in another vein.

On Aug. 5 the length of the Five-Cent Library stories was cut from 30,000 words to 20,000, and the remuneration was cut from $50 to $40. Another juvenile paper was started and Edwards was asked to submit serials for it. In fact, 1901 might be called a "boom" year for the Fiction Factory, although the returns, while satisfactory, were not of the "boom" variety.

Perhaps the reader may remember the serial, "A Vassar Girl," referred to in a previous chapter as having been submitted to Harte & Perkins and rejected. Edwards had faith in this story and offered it to Mr. White. Mr. White's judgment, however, tallied with that of Harte & Perkins. Under date of June 13 Mr. White wrote:

"I am sorry that 'A Vassar Girl' has not borne out the promise of the opening chapters. The interest in it is not sufficiently *sustained* for serial use. The story might be divided into several incidents, which do not grow inevitably the one out of the other. For this reason it has, as a whole, proved disappointing and I am returning the manuscript by express. We should be glad, however, to have you continue to submit work to us."

With faith undiminished, Edwards forwarded the story to McClure's Newspaper Syndicate. It was returned without an explanation of any kind. Again he prevailed upon Harte & Perkins to consider it. It came back from them on Sept. 13, with this message:

"I am sorry to say that we do not feel inclined to revise our judgement with reference to your manuscript story, 'A Vassar Girl.' I am inclined to think from looking over the review of the story that it would be well for you to sell it just as it is, and we hope you will be able to find a market for it somewhere. It would not pay us to publish."

Edwards knew that the story, wrought out of his Arizona experiences, was true in local color and good of its kind, and he failed to understand why it was not appreciated. Then, on Sep. 14, came this from the S. S. McClure Company:

"During July we had under consideration a story of yours entitled, 'A Vassar Girl.' On July 31 we wrote you from the Syndicate, informing you that we hoped to be able to use the story as a serial in the very near future. The serial was taken back for consideration in the book department by one of the readers who wished again to examine it, and from there it was erroneously returned to you. Now if you have not disposed of the serial rights of 'A Vassar Girl' we should like you again to forward the story to us, and we will submit it to some of our papers as we had always intended to do. We will then give you a prompt decision."

The story was purchased, and Edwards' faith in it was confirmed.

It was during this year of 1901 that Edwards had a fleeting glimpse of fortune as a playwright. His story, "The Tangle in Butte," had been read by an actor, a leading man in a Kansas City stock company, who wanted dramatic rights so that he might have a play taken from it and written around him. Edwards proposed to write the play himself. He did so, and was promptly offered $5,000 for the play, payable in installments after production. Following a good deal of correspondence it was decided to put on the piece for a week's try-out in Kansas City. Edwards waived his right to royalties for the week, models of the scenery were made, rehearsals began—and then the actor was suddenly stricken with a serious illness and the deal was off. When he had recovered sufficiently to travel he went East, taking the play with him. For several months he tried to interest various managers in it, but without effect.

The year 1901 closed for Edwards with the sketches for the trade paper no longer in demand; but, otherwise, be faced a steadily brightening prospect for the Fiction Factory.

```
1900:
Circus Series, 28 @ $40 each...........................$1120.00
Circus Series, Completing unfinished story ............   20.00
Five-Cent Library, 23 @ $40 each......................  920.00
Trade Paper Sketches, 10 @ $10 each...............  100.00
"He Was A Stranger," .........................  250.00
"The Man From Dakota," .........................  200.00
"What Happened to the Colonel," .................   75.00

          Total ...................................................$2685.00
1901:
Five-Cent Library, 10 rewritten @ $30 each..........$  300.00
Five-Cent Library, 8 @ $50 each ...................  400.00
Five-Cent Library, 16 @ $40 each...................  640.00
Four Boys' Serials @ $100 each.....................  400.00
"The Tangle in Butte," ...........................  200.00
"Tale of Two Towns," ...........................  150.00
"A Vassar Girl," ................................................  100.00
Trade Paper Sketches, 9 @ $10 each...............   90.00

          Total ..........................................................  $2280.00
```

Very Often.

———

Poeta nascitur; non fit. This has been somewhat freely translated by one who should know, as "The poet is born; not paid."

XV.

FROM THE
FACTORY'S FILES

A letter of commendation from the reader of a story to the writer is not only a pleasant thing in itself but it proves the reader a person of noble soul and high motives. *Noblesse oblige!*

The writer who loves his work is not of a sordid nature. The check an editor sends him for his story is the smallest part of his reward. His has been the joy to create, to see a thought take form and amplify under the spell of his inspiration. A joy which is scarcely less is to know that his work has been appreciated by others.

A letter like the one below, for instance, not only gives pleasure to the recipient but at the same time fires a writer with determination never to let his work fall short of a previous performance. This reader's good will he *must* keep, at all hazards.

"Wayland, N. Y., March 22nd, 1905.
"Mr. John Milton Edwards,
    Care The F. A. Munsey Co., New York.
My dear Sir:
    I read the story in this last *Argosy,* entitled 'Fate and the Figure Seven,' and was in a way considering if it were possible that a man could act in the subconscious state you picture. Deem my surprise, last night, when I read of a similar case in the report of the Brockton accident.
    In case you should have failed to notice this item, I send you a clipping from a Buffalo paper.
    I WISH INCIDENTALLY TO THANK YOU FOR YOUR SHARE IN MAKING LIFE PLEASANT FOR ME. I have enjoyed your works immensely from time to time on

account of their decidedly original ideas. They are always refreshingly out of the ordinary rut. Yours truly,
"A. F. V———."

There is one sentence in this letter which Edwards has put in capitals. If possible, he would have written it in letters of gold. In this little world, so crowded with sorrow and tragedy, what is it worth to have had a share in making life pleasant for a stranger? To Edwards it has been worth infinitely more than he received for "Fate and the Figure Seven."

Another letter carries an equally pleasant message:

"Livingstone, Montana, Sep. 16, 1903.
"Mr. John Milton Edwards,
Care The Argosy, New York City.
Dear Sir:
Having read your former stories in *The Argosy* on Arizona, and last night having commenced 'The Grains of Gold,' I trust you will pardon my expression of appreciation of said stories. I lived ten years in Arizona as private secretary to several of the Federal Judges, and also lived in Mexico, and am still familiar with conditions in that section.

I have enjoyed most keenly your handling of thrilling scenes on Arizona soil. It is an exasperation that they appear in serial form, as I dislike the month's interval.

My only purpose in writing is to express my admiration of your plots and local color, and I remain,
Sincerely yours,
"Richard S. S———."

Edwards has always prided himself on keeping true to the actual conditions of the country which forms the screen against which his plot and characters are thrown. This is a gratifying tribute, therefore, from one who knows.

A letter which rather startled Edwards, suggesting as it did the Maricopa Indian incident which trailed upon the heels of "A Study in Red," is this:

"Colorado Springs, Colo., 2-25-'09.

Mr. John Milton Edwards,

Dear Sir: Through the kindness of the editor of the *Blue Book* I received your address. I am very much interested in your story entitled, 'Country Rock at Kish-Kish,' and know the greater part of it to be true to life, but would like to know if it is ALL true. Did Sager have a daughter? And where did Sager go when he left Arizona? Or is that just a part of the story? I am very much interested in that character, Sager. Can you tell me if he is still living, and where? Any information that you may be able to give me will be more than appreciated.

Thanking you in advance for the favor, I am,

Yours respectfully,

Mrs. James R. S———."

Edwards answered this letter—he answers promptly all such letters that come to him and esteems it a privilege—and received a reply. It appeared that Mrs. S— was the grand-daughter of a man whom "Sager" had robbed of a large amount of money. "Country Rock at Kish-Kish" was built on a newspaper clipping twenty years old. This clipping Edwards forwarded to Mrs. S— in the hope that it might help her in her quest for "Sager." The letter was returned as uncalled for. Should this ever fall under the eye of Mrs. S— she will understand that Edwards did everything in his power to be of assistance to her.

Now and again a letter, which compliments an author indirectly, will chasten his mounting spirit with the reminder of a "slip:"

"Rochester, N. Y., Nov. 17, 1905.

"Mr. John Milton Edwards:

Dear Sir:—Will you please tell me where I can get more of your stories than in the *Argosy;* and also, in reference to your story which concludes in December *Argosy,* how many large autos were in use in New York in 1892?

Yours respectfully,

"Howard Z———."

Carelessness in a writer is inexcusable. It is the one thing which a reader will not forgive, for it is very apt to spoil his pleasure in what would otherwise have been a good story. This is a sublimated form of the "gold-brick game," inasmuch as the reader pays his money for a magazine only to find that he has been "buncoed" by the table of contents. If there is a flaw in the factory's product, rest assured that it will be discovered and react to the disadvantage of everything else that comes from the same mill.

Many readers will be found whose interest in a writer's work is so keen that they are tempted to offer suggestions. Such suggestions are not to be lightly considered. Magazines are published to please their readers, and they are successful in a direct ratio with their ability to accomplish this end. Naturally, the old doggerel concerning "many men of many minds" will apply here, and a single suggestion that has not a wide appeal, or that fails to conform to the policy of the magazine, must be handled with great care.

"Cincinnati, Ohio, Oct. 31, 1905.

"Mr. John Milton Edwards,
    Care Frank A. Munsey Co.,
        New York.
Dear Sir:
    Because of the increasing interest in Socialism, would it not be a good idea to write a story showing under what conditions we should live in, say, the year 2,000, if the Socialists should come into power?
    You might begin your story with the United States under a Socialistic form of government, and later on Socialize the rest of the world.
    Your imaginative stories are the ones most eagerly sought in the pages of *The Argosy,* and I think that a story such as I have suggested would serve to increase your popularity among the readers of fiction.   Sincerely yours,
                                    "J. H. S———."

It frequently happens that a comedian will get after a writer with a stuffed club or a slapstick. Some anonymous humorist, upon reading a story of Edwards' in *The Argosy,* labored and brought forth the following:

"John Milton Edwards,   "November 19,1904.
   Care Frank A. Munsey Co.,
     New York.
My dear John :—

   I have read with much pleasure and delight the first six chapters of your latest story, 'At Large in Terra Incognita,' as published in the December number of *The Argosy.*

   I cannot understand why you failed to send me the proof-sheets of this story for correction, as you did with 'There and Back.' It is evident so far as I have read the person who corrected your proof-sheets was as ignorant as yourself.

   Where you got the material for this story is not within my memory, retrospective though it is, and I am sure you must have been on one of your periodical drunks, otherwise the flights of fancy you have taken would have been more rational and not so far removed beyond the pale of the human intellect.

   Now, my dear John, I beg of you to give up going on these habitual tears, because you are not only ruining your constitution but your reputation as a writer is having reflections cast upon it. I trust you will not take this letter as a sermon but rather in a spirit of friendly counsel.

   I hope you will send me at once the remaining chapters of this great 'At Large in Terra Incognita.'
              Your Nemesis,
                "Theo. Roosenfeldt,
                Pres't Trust-Busters' Asso."

Readers have usually the courage of their convictions and not many anonymous letters find their way into the office of the Fiction Factory. Edwards remembers one other letter which was signed "Biff A. Hiram." At that time Edwards did not know Mr. Biff A. Hiram from Adam, but he has since made the gentleman's acquaintance, and discovered how wide is his circle of friends.

If praise from a reader has a tendency to exalt, then how much more of the flattering unction may a writer lay to his soul when approval comes from a brother or sister of the pen? With such a letter, this brief symposium from the Factory files may be brought to a close.

"Mr. John Milton Edwards,
Dear Sir:—

Allow me to congratulate you upon your success with the novelette in a recent issue of the *Blue Book*. It is to my mind the BEST short story of its kind I have EVER read. As I try to write short stories I see its merits doubly. The modelling is splendid. Will you pardon my display of interest?   Very truly yours,

"K. B———."

Rules for Authors.

Dr. Edward Everett Hale, author of "The Man without a Country," and other notable books, gives a few rules which are of interest to the author and the journalist. Dr. Hale's success in the literary world makes these rules, gleaned from the field of experience, especially valuable to young writers:

1. Know what you want to say.

2. Say it.

3. Use your own language.

4. Leave out all fine phrases.

5. A short word is better than a long one.

6. The fewer words, other things being equal, the better.

7. Cut it to pieces—which means revise, revise, revise.

XVI.

GROWING
PROSPERITY

The years 1902 and 1903 were busier years than ever for the Fiction Factory. Nineteen-two is to be remembered particularly for opening a new departure in the story line in *The Argosy*, and for placing the first book with the G. W. Dillingham Company. Nineteen-three claims distinction for seeing the book brought out and for boosting the Factory returns beyond the three-thousand-dollar mark. But it must not be inferred that the book had very much to do with this. Edwards' royalties for the year were less than $100.

In September, 1902, Edwards made one of his customary "prospecting" trips to New York. If there was anything in omens his stay in the city promised dire things. On the second day after his arrival he went to Coney Island with a friend. Together they called on the seventh son of a seventh son and had their palms read. The dispenser of occult knowledge assured Edwards that the future was *very* bright, that Tuesday was his lucky day and that Spring was the best time for him to consummate his business undertakings. That day, as it happened, was Tuesday. In the teeth of this promising augury, and within ten minutes after leaving the palmist's booth, some Coney Island "dip" shattered Edwards' confidence in Tuesday by annexing his wallet. The wallet, as it happened, contained all the money Edwards had brought from home, with the exception of a little loose change.

This was the second time Edwards had been all but stranded in the Metropolis, and this time the stranding was more complete. When he cast up accounts that evening he found himself with a cash balance of $1.63. Fortunately Mrs. Edwards was not along. He had left her at home with the understanding that she was to come on later. When a writer has come within hailing distance of the bread line there remains but one thing to do, and that is to start the Factory going with day and night shifts.

Edwards called on Mr. White, of *The Argosy,* and outlined a serial story. He was told to go ahead with it. For five days Edwards hardly stirred from his room. At the end of that time he had completed "The Desperado's Understudy," and had sold it to Mr. White for $250, spot cash.

After completing this serial, Edwards outlined to Mr. White a novelette which would furnish *The Argosy* with something new in the fiction line. The plot was based on a musical extravaganza which he had written, several years before, in collaboration with Mr. Eugene Kaeuffer, at one time connected with *The Bostonians.* Nothing had ever come of this ambitious effort, although book and musical score were completed and offered to Mr. McDonald of *The Bostonians* and to Mr. Thomas Q. Seabrooke. Mr. White liked the idea of the story immensely and gave Edwards *carte blanche* to go ahead with it.

This story, "Ninety, North," paved the way for other fantastic yarns which made a decided hit in *The Argosy* and so pointed Edwards along a fresh line of endeavor which proved as congenial as it was profitable.

Several months before he visited New York Edwards had sold to The McClure Syndicate, a juvenile serial which may be referred to here as "The Campaign at Topeka." For this he had been offered $200, which offer he promptly accepted. He had not received a check, however, and was at a loss to understand the reason. To this day the reason remains obscure, although later events pointed to a misunderstanding of some kind regarding the story between the Syndicate and one of its readers. Before Edwards left New York he was paid the $200. More than a year afterward he was informed that the serial had been sold to the Century Company for *St. Nicholas,* and that after publication in that magazine it was to be brought out in book form.

It was Mr. T. C. McClure who put Edwards in touch with the Dillingham Company and referred him to them as prospective publishers, in cloth, of the successful Syndicate story, "A Tale of Two Towns." Edwards submitted galley proofs of the serial to Mr. Cook of the Dillingham Company, and ultimately signed a contract to have the book published on the usual royalty basis of ten per cent.

For Harte & Perkins, during the year, the Factory ground out nickel novels, juvenile serials, one sketch for the trade paper and a few detective stories. On Nov. 28, after he had returned home from New York, he was notified:

"Much as I regret to inform you of it, by a recent purchase of copyright stories we are placed in a position where we will not require any further material for any of our five-cent libraries for some time to come, so we must discontinue orders to you for all this material."

Edwards, in a way, had become hardened to messages of this kind. *The Argosy* was an anchor to windward, and he resolved to give his attention to serials for Mr. White. In December, 1902, and January and February, 1903, he wrote and forwarded "Ninety, North," a second fantastic story called "There and Back," and the Arizona serial "Grains of Gold." All three of these stories were sold at once, bringing in $700. In a letter dated Oct. 14, 1903, Mr. White had this to say about "There and Back:"

"Thanks for letting me see the enclosed letter regarding 'Ninety, North.' I am equally pleased with yourself at its significance. I am wondering whether you have heard much about your story 'There and Back?' My impression is that that has been one of the most popular stories you have ever written for *The Argosy*. When I see you I will tell you an odd little circumstance that occurred in connection with its run in the magazine."

The circumstances referred to by Mr. White took place in Paris. One of *The Argosy's* readers happened to be in a café, looking over proofs of a forthcoming installment of "There and Back" while at her luncheon, when she heard the story being discussed, in complimentary terms, by a number of Frenchmen at an adjoining table. Strange indeed that Frenchmen should be interested in an American story, and stranger still that *The Argosy's* reader should be reading an installment of the very same story while men in that foreign café were discussing it!

The first installment of "There and Back," Mr. White informed Edwards, had increased *The Argosy's* circulation *seven thousand copies.**

On March 2 Harte & Perkins requested Edwards to continue work on the old Five-Cent Library. By taking up this work again he would be diminishing the Factory's serial output, but he reflected that his fertility in the matter of serials would soon have Mr. White over-supplied. Therefore Edwards decided to go on with the nickel weeklies.

In March, as Mr. MacLean of *The Popular Magazine* once put it, Edwards "came out in cloth," the Dillingham Company issuing "A Tale of Two Towns" on St. Patrick's Day.

What are the feelings of an author when he opens his first book for the first time? If you, dear reader, are yet to "get out in cloth" for the first time, then some day you will know. But, if you value your peace of mind, do not build too gorgeous an air castle on the foundation of this printed thing. Printed things are at the mercy of the reviewers and, in a larger sense, of the great reading public. The reviewers, in nearly every instance, were kind with "A Tale of Two Towns." In many quarters it was praised fulsomely, but the book did not strike that fickle sentiment called popular fancy. In six months, Mr. Cook, of the Dillingham Company, wrote Edwards that "A Tale of Two Towns" was "a dead duck." In the December settlement, however, the remains yielded royalties of $96.60. For two or three

---

*"There and Back" went through the Fiction Factory in twelve days.

years the royalties trailed along, and finally the edition was wound up with a payment of $1.50. *Sic transit gloria!*

During January, 1903, a theatrical gentleman requested Edwards to dramatize a book which Messrs. Street & Smith had issued in paper covers. "You can change the title," the gentleman suggested, "and slightly change the incidents. In that way it won't be necessary to write Street & Smith for permission or, indeed, to let them know anything about it." Edwards knew, however, that nothing will so surely wreck a writer's prospects as playing fast and loose with editors and publishers. He refused to consider the theatrical gentleman's proposition. Instead, he forwarded his *Argosy* story, "The Desperado's Understudy," upon which Mr. White had given him dramatic rights, and offered to make a stage version of it. The offer was accepted and a play was built up from the story. The theatrical gentleman was pleased and said he would give $1,500 for the dramatization. Then, alas! the theatrical gentleman's company went on the rocks at the Alhambra Theatre, in Chicago, and Edwards had repeated his former playwriting experience.

The two years' work figured out in this wise:

1902:

23 Five-Cent Libraries @ $40 each	$ 920.00
8 detective stories @ $40 each	320.00
4 juvenile serials @ $100 each	400.00
1 sketch for trade paper	10.00
"The Desperado's Understudy,"	250.00
"The Campaign at Topeka,"	200.00
Short stories	67.00
Total.	$2167.00

1903:

42 Five-Cent Libraries @ $40 each $1680.00
 2 detective stories @ $40 each 80.00
"Ninety, North," 150.00
"There and Back," 250.00
"A Sensational Affair," short story,.................. 15.00
"Grains of Gold," 300.00
"Fate's Gamblers," *................................. 100.00
"The Morning Star Race," short story, ... 15.00
"A Game for Two," 200.00
Royalties on book, "A Tale of Two Towns,".......... 96.60
"The Point of Honor," 150.00

Total. $3036.60

*This story sold through Kellogg Newspaper Company, Chicago. The two short stories sold to the late lamented *Wayside Tales,* Detroit, Mich.

As several gentlemen in these times, by the wonderful force of genius only, without the least assistance of learning, perhaps without being able to read, have made a considerable figure in the republic of letters; the modern critics, I am told, have lately begun to assert, that all kind of learning is entirely useless to a writer, and indeed, no other than a kind of fetters on the natural sprightliness and activity of the imagination, which is thus weighed down, and prevented from soaring to those high flights which otherwise it would be able to reach.

This doctrine, I am afraid, is at present carried much too far; for why should writing differ so much from other arts? The nimbleness of a dancing-master is not at all prejudiced by being taught to move; nor doth any mechanic, I believe, excercise his tools the worse by having learnt to use them.—*Fielding,* "Tom Jones."

XVII.

ETHICS OF THE NICKEL NOVEL

Is the nickel novel easy to write? The writer who has never attempted one is quite apt to think that it is. There are hundreds of writers, the Would-be-Goods, making less than a thousand a year, who would throw up their hands in horror at the very thought of debasing their art by contriving at "sensational" five-cent fiction. So far from "debasing their art," as a matter of fact they could not lift it to the *high plane* of the nickel novel if they tried. Of these Would-be-Goods more anon—to use an expression of the ante-bellum romancers. Suffice to state, in this place, writers of recognized standing, and even ministers, have written—and some now are writing—these quick-moving stories. There's a knack about it, and the knack is not easy to acquire. No less a person than Mr. Richard Duffy, formerly editor of *Ainslee's* and later of the *Cavalier,* a man of rare gifts as a writer, once told Edwards that the nickel novel was beyond his powers.

So far as Edwards is concerned, he gave the best that was in him to the half-dime "dreadfuls," and he made nothing dreadful of them after all. He has written hundreds, and there is not a line in any one of them which he would not gladly have his own son read. In fact, his ethical standard, to which every story must measure up, was expressed in this mental question as he worked: "If I had a boy would I willingly put this before him?"

If the answer was No, the incident, the paragraph, the sentence or the word was eliminated. In 1910 Edwards wrote his last nickel novel, turning his back deliberately on three thousand dollars a year (they were paying him $60 each for them then), not because they were "debasing his art" but because he could make more money at other writing—for when one is forty-four he must get on as fast as he can.

The libraries, as they were written by Edwards, were typed on paper 8½" by 13," the marginal stops so placed that a typewritten line approximated the same line when printed. Eighty of these sheets completed a story, and five pages were regularly allowed to each chapter. Thus there were always sixteen chapters in every story.

First it is necessary to submit titles, and scenes for illustration. Selecting an appropriate title is an art in itself. Alliteration is all right, if used sparingly, and novel effects that do not defy the canons of good taste should be sought after. The title, too, should go hand in hand with the picture that illustrates the story. This picture, by the way, has demands of its own. In the better class of nickel novels firearms and other deadly weapons are tabooed. The picture must be unusual and it must be exciting, but its suggested morality must he high.

The ideas for illustrations all go to the artist days or even weeks in advance of the stories themselves. It is the writer's business to lay out this prospective work intelligently, so that he may weave around it a group of logical stories.

Usually the novels are written in sets of three; that is, throughout such a series the same principal characters are used, and three different groups of incidents are covered. In this way, while each story is complete in itself, it is possible to combine the series and preserve the effect of a single story from beginning to end. These sets are so combined, as a matter of fact, and sold for ten cents.

Each chapter closes with a "curtain." In other words, the chapter works the action up to an interesting point, similar to a serial "leave-off," and drops a quick curtain. Skill is important here. The publishers of this class of fiction will not endure inconsistency for a moment. The stories appeal to a clientele keen to detect the improbable and to treat it with contempt.

Good, snappy dialogue is favored, but it must be dialogue that moves the story along. An apt retort has no excuse in the yarn unless it really belongs there. A multitude of incidents—none of them hackneyed—is a prime requisite. Complexity of plot invites censure—and usually secures it. The plot must be simple, but it must be striking.

One author failed because he had his hero-detective strain his massive intellect through 20,000 words merely to recover $100 that had been purloined from an old lady's handbag. If the author had made it a million dollars stolen from a lady like Mrs. Hetty Green, probably his labor would have been crowned with success. These five-cent heroes are in no sense small potatoes. They may court perils galore and rub elbows with death, now and then, for nothing at all, but certainly never for the mere bagatelle of $100.

The hero does not drink, He does not swear. Very often he will not smoke. He is a chivalrous gentleman, ever a friend of the weak and deserving. He accomplishes all this with a ready good nature that has nothing of the goody-good in its make-up. The hero does not smoke because, being an athlete, he must keep in constant training in order to master his many difficulties. For the same reason he will not drink. As for swearing, it is a useless pastime and very common; besides, it betrays excitement, and the hero is never excited.

The old-style yellow-back hero was given to massacres. He slew his enemies valiantly by brigades. Not so the modern hero of the five-cent novel. Rarely, in the stories, does any one cross the divide. And whenever the villain is hurt, he is quite apt to recover, thank the hero for hurting him—and become his sworn friend.

The story must be *clean,* and while it must necessarily be exciting, it must yet leave the reader's mind with a net profit in all the manly virtues. Is this easy?

Please note this extract from a letter written by Harte & Perkins Dec. 25, 1902—it covers a point whose humor, Edwards thought, drew the sting of dishonesty:

Your last story, No. 285, opened well, had plenty of good incidents and was interesting, but there are several points in which it might have been improved.

Your description of Two Spot's scheme of posing Dutchy as a petrified boy is amusing, but the plan was dishonest and a piece of trickery. It was all right, perhaps, to let the boys go ahead without the knowledge of the Hero, but when he learned of it he should have put a stop to the plan immediately. It was all right to have him laugh at it, but at the same time he should have spoken severely to the boys about it and ordered them to return the money they had received through their trick. He did not do this in your story and it was necessary for me to alter it considerably in the first part on that account.

The Hero is supposed to be the soul of honor, and in your story he is posed as a party to a deception practised on the citizens of Ouray, by which they were defrauded of the money they paid for admission to see the supposed "petrified boy." Such conduct on his part would soon lose for him the admiration of the readers of the weekly, as it places him on a moral level, almost, with the robbers whom he is bringing to justice."

Consider that, you Would-be-Goods, who are not above putting worse things in your "high-class" work. And can you say "I am holier than thou" to the conscientious writer who turns out his 20,000 or 25,000 words a week along these ethical lines? Handsome is as handsome does!

Somebody is going to write these stories. There is a demand for them. The writer who can set hand to such fiction, who meets his moral responsibilities unflinchingly, is doing a splendid work for Young America.

And yet, as stated in a previous chapter, there are nickel novels *and* nickel novels—some to read and some to put in the stove unread. High-minded publishers, however, are not furnishing the careful head of the family with material for his kitchen fire.

It costs you nothing to think, but it costs infinitely to write. I therefore preach to you eternally that art of writing which Boileau has so well known and so well taught, that respect for the language, that connection and sequence of ideas, that air of ease with which he conducts his readers, that naturalness which is the true fruit of art, and that appearance of facility which is due to toil alone. A word out of place spoils the most beautiful thought.—*Voltaire to Helvetius*, a young author.

XVIII

KEEPING
EVERLASTINGLY AT IT

Edwards had not visited New York in 1903, but he landed there on Friday, Jan. 1, 1904,—literally storming in on a train that was seven hours late on account of the weather. A cab hurried him and his wife to the place in Forty-fourth street where the pleasant landlady used to hold forth, but they found, alas! that the old stamping ground was in the hands of strangers. It was like being turned away from home.

Where should they go? Edwards remembered that, on one of his previous visits to New York, Mr. Perkins had recommended the St. George Hotel, over in Brooklyn. The St. George was within a few blocks of the south end of the bridge and the offices of Harte & Perkins were in William street, close to the north end. So Edwards and his wife went to the Brooklyn hotel and there established their headquarters.

On Jan. 2 Edwards called on the patrons of his Factory. The result was not particluarly encouraging. Harte & Perkins instructed him to stop work on the Five-Cent Library, but said that in about two months they would have a new library for him to take care of.

Edwards had brought with him to the city his dramatic version of "The Tangle in Butte," the play which had come so near turning $5,000 into the Factory's strong-box. It was Edward's hope that he might be able to dispose of the play, but the hope went glimmering when he learned that there were 10,000 actors stranded in New York, and that things theatrical were generally in a bad way.

During 1903 Edwards had corresponded with Mr. H. H. Lewis, editor of *The Popular Magazine*, a recent venture of Messrs. Street & Smith's. He had submitted manuscripts to Mr. Lewis but they had not proved to be in line with *The Popular's* requirements. It is difficult, through correspondence, to discover just what an editor wants. The only way to get at such a thing properly is by personal interview. If the would-be contributor does not then get the editor's needs clearly in mind it is his own fault.

Edwards called on Mr. Lewis and had a pleasant chat with him. The assistant editor was Mr. A. D. Hall, a capable gentleman who had been with Messrs. Street & Smith for many years, and with whom Edwards was well acquainted.

At that time Louis Joseph Vance was writing for *The Popular Magazine*, among others, and Edwards met him in Mr. Lewis' office. As Edwards was leaving, after outlining a novelette and receiving a commission to write it, he paused with one hand on the door-knob.

"I'll turn in the story, Mr. Lewis," said he, "and I hope you'll like it and buy it."

"Of course he'll like it and buy it," called out Vance. "You're going to write it for him, aren't you?"

"Why, yes," returned Edwards, "but—"

"You're not a peddler," interrupted Vance, "to write stuff and go hawking it about from office to office. We're writers, and when we know what a man wants *we deliver the goods.*"

This was before the days of "The Brass Bowl" and *"Terence O'Rourke,"* but already Vance had found himself and was striking the key-note of confidence. *Confidence*—that's the word. Back it up with fair ability and the writer will go far.

From *The Popular's* editorial rooms Edwards went up Fifth avenue for a call on the editor of *The Argosy.* Much to his disappointment Mr. White was out of town for New Year's and would not return until the following week.

The story which Edwards had presented to Mr. Lewis in its oral and tabloid form was one that had been written in 1903 and turned down by Mr. White. Before offering the manuscript to *The Popular,* Edwards intended to rewrite it and strengthen it.

A typewriter was ordered sent over to the St. George Hotel, and on Jan. 3 the rewriting of the novelette was begun. The story was called "The Highwayman's Waterloo," or something to that effect. On the following day twenty-four pages of the manuscript were submitted to Mr. Lewis, won his approval, and the rewriting proceeded.

Two chapters of a serial were also offered to Mr. White for examination. The story was called "The Skirts of Chance," and had been begun before Edwards left home.

During 1902 and '03 Edwards had worked, at odd times, on what he designed to be a "high-class" juvenile story. It was 60,000 words in length, when completed in the Summer of 1903, and in September he had submitted it to Dodd, Mead & Company. Not having heard from the story, on this January day that saw him passing out fragments of manuscripts to *The Popular* and *The Argosy* he went on farther up Fifth avenue and dropped in to ask D., M. & Co., how "Danny W.," was fareing at the hands of their readers. He was told that five readers had examined the story and that it was then in the hands of the sixth! Some of the readers—and this came to him privately—had turned in a favorable report. Because of this, the author of "Danny W.," went back to Brooklyn considerably elated. It would be an honor indeed to have the book break through such a formidable brigade of readers and get into the catalogue of the good old house of Dodd, Mead & Company.

The "highwayman" novelette was finished and submitted in its complete form on Jan. 6. On the same day Mr. White informed Edwards that he was well pleased with the two chapters of "The Skirts of Chance" and told him to proceed with it.

Fortune was on the upward trend for Edwards, and he was sent for by Dodd, Mead & Company, on Jan. 15, and informed that they would either bring out "Danny W.," on a royalty or pay a cash price for the book rights. Edwards, remembering his disastrous publishing experience with "A Tale of Two Towns," accepted $200 in cash.

Mr. Lewis bought the novelette for $125, and Harte & Perkins, on the same day, gave Edwards a new library to do—35,000 words in each story at $50.

Complete manuscript of "The Skirts of Chance" was submitted to Mr. White on Jan. 22, and on Jan. 27 Edwards received $300 for it.

By Feb. 8 Edwards had written and sold to Mr. Lewis another novelette entitled, "The Duke's Understudy," for which he received $140.

On Feb. 9 he and his wife returned to Michigan. Edwards had been in New York forty days and had gathered in $965. He left New York with orders for *Argosy* serials and with the new library, "Sea and Shore," to be turned in at the rate of one story every two months.

In May he was requested to go on with the Old Five-Cent Library. These stories were forwarded regularly one each week, until November, when orders were again discontinued.

In September, "Danny W.," appeared. As with "A Tale of Two Towns," the reviewers were more than kind to "Danny W.," and there is just a possibility that they killed him with kindness. The idea obtains, in supposedly well-informed circles, that the only way for reviewers to help a book is to damm it utterly. Be this as it may, although illustrated in color and put out in the best style of the book-maker's art, "Danny W.," did not prove much of a success. A California paper bought serial rights on the story for $50, and thus the book netted the author, all told, the modest sum of $250.

During this year, also, The A. N. Kellogg Newspaper Company sold serial rights on "Fate's Gamblers" for $30, took 50 per cent. as a commission and presented Edwards with what was left.

A short story, "The Camp Coyote," was sold to Mr. Titherington, for *Munsey's;* and Edwards had opened a new market in Street & Smith's magazines. Thus was brought to a close a fairly prosperous year.

In 1905 the returns slid backward a little. During this year, and the year preceding, some stories which had failed with Mr. White were received with favor by Mr.

Kerr, of *The Chicago Ledger*—at the *Ledger* price, ranging from $30 upward to $75.

The *Woman's Home Companion,* to which Edwards had vainly tried to sell serial rights on "Danny W.," accepted a two-part story entitled, "The Redskin and the Paper-Talk," and paid $200 for it. This is the story of which a chapter was lost in the composing room, and Edwards received an honorarium of $5 for having a carbon duplicate of the few missing pages.

In 1905, also, The American Press Association did business with Edwards to the amount of $30. Another market for the Edward's product—worth mentioning even though the amount of business done was not large.

The returns for the two years were as follows:

1904:
"The Highwayman's Waterloo," .... $ 125.00
"Danny W.," 200.00
"Danny W.," serial rights 50.00
"The Skirts of Chance," 300.00
"The Duke's Understudy," 140.00
"At Large in Terra Incognita," 175.00
"The Man from the Stone Age," short story.......... 25.00
"The Honorable Jim," 250.00
"Fate's Gamblers," serial rights..................... 15.00
"A Deal with Destiny," 150.00
"The Enchanted Ranch," 75.00
"The Camp Coyote," 40.00
"Under the Ban," 75.00
"A Master of Graft," 225.00
26 Five-Cent Libraries @ $40 each 1040.00
4 Sea and Shore Libraries @ 50 each 200.00

    Total. $3085.00

1905:
"Cornering Boreas," short story .... $ 30.00
"The Redskin and the Paper-talk," 200.00
"The Redskin and the Paper-talk," additional pay't.... 5.00
"Mountebank's Dilemma," short story................ 25.00
"Helping Columbus," 350.00
"The Edge of the Sword," 200.00

"Yellow Clique,"	100.00
"A Mississippi Snarl,"	200.00
"The Black Box,"	200.00
"A Wireless Wooing," short story	15.00
"The Freelance,"	50.00
"The Luck of Bill Lattimer,"	30.00
"Machine-made Road-agent," short story	15.00
"The Man from Mars,"	275.00
10 Sea and Shore stories @ $50 each	500.00
Total.	$2195.00

Good, philosophical Ras Wilson once said to a new reporter, "Young man, write as you feel, but try to feel right. Be good humored toward every one and everything. Believe that other folks are just as good as you are, for they are. Give 'em your best and bear in mind that God has sent them, in his wisdom, all the trouble they need, and it is for you to scatter gladness and decent, helpful things as you go. Don't be particular about how the stuff will look in print, but let'er go. Some one will understand. That is better than to write so dash bing high, or so tarnashun deep, that no one understands. Let'er go."

There was once a poor man hounded to death by creditors. Ruin and suicide vied for his surrender. But he was a man of the twentieth century, and flippantly but with unbounded faith he collected a few odd pennies and hied him to a newspaper office. Stopping scarcely to frame his sentence he inserted a "want" advertisement, stating his circumstances and declaring he would commit suicide unless aid was proffered. Within twenty-four hours he had $250; before another sun his employer advanced as much more. Carefully advising the newspaper to discontinue the advertisement, he paid off his creditors— and lived happily ever afterward! No, this is not a fairy tale. The time was a few weeks ago, the city Chicago and the newspaper, *The Tribune*. The moral is, that originality in writing, coupled with a fresh idea, brings a check.

XIX.

LOVE YOUR WORK
FOR THE
WORK'S SAKE

The sentiment which Edwards has tried to carry through every paragraph and line of this book is this, that "Writing is its own reward." His meaning is, that to the writer the joy of the work is something infinitely higher, finer and more satisfying than its pecuniary value to the editor who buys it. Material success, of course, is a necessity, unless—happy condition!—the writer has a private income on which to draw for meeting the sordid demands of life. But this also is true: A writer even of modest talent will have material success in a direct ratio with the joy he finds in his work!—Because, brother of the pen, when one takes pleasure in an effort, then that effort attracts merit inevitably. If any writing is a merciless grind the result will show it—and the editor will see it, and reject.

There are times, however, when doubt shakes the firmest confidence. A writer will have moods into which will creep a distrust of the work upon which he is at that moment engaged. If necessity spurs him on and he cannot rise above his misgivings, the story will testify to the lack of faith, doubts will increase as defects multiply and the story will be ruined. THE WRITER MUST HAVE FAITH IN HIS WORK QUITE APART FROM THE MONEY HE EXPECTS TO RECEIVE FOR IT. If he has this faith he reaches toward a spiritual success beside which the highest material success is paltry indeed.

When a writer sits down to a story let him blind his eyes to the financial returns, even though they may be sorely needed. Let him forget that his wares are to be offered for sale, and consider them as being wrought for his own diversion. Let him say to himself, "I shall make this the best story I have ever written; I shall weave my soul into its warp and whether it sells or not I shall be satisfied to know that I have put upon paper the BEST that is in me." If he will do this, he will achieve a spiritual success and—as surely as day follows night—a material success beyond his fondest dreams. BUT he must keep his eye single to the TRUE success and must have no commerce in thought with what may come to him materially.

To some, all this may appear too idealistic, too transcendental. There are natures so worldly, perhaps even among writers, as to scoff at the idea of spiritual success. They are overshadowed by the Material, and when the Spiritual, which is the true source of their power, is no longer the "still, small voice" of their inspiration, they will be bankrupt materially as well.

A writer cannot hide himself in his work. His individuality is written into it, and he may be read between the lines for what he is. A creation reflects the creator, and that the work may be good the writer should have spiritual ideals and do his utmost to live up to them. Let him have a purpose, be it never so humble, to benefit in some way his fellow-man, and let him hew steadily to the line. Love your work for the work's sake and material benefits "will be added unto you."

Years ago Edwards found an article in a newspaper that appealed to him powerfully. He clipped it out, preserved it and has made it of great help in his writing. It is a wonderful "Doubt-destroyer." In the hope that it may be an inspiration to others, he reproduces it here:

STANDARDS OF SUCCESS.

At a time when material success is so generally regarded as the chief goal of human effort it is interesting to find a man in Professor Hadley's position presenting arguments for a broader view of the question. In his baccalaureate sermon the president of Yale offered the graduates some advice which at least they should find stimulating. He does not discredit or discourage the ambition for practical success but he makes it plain that in his view there is danger in measuring success in life "by the concrete results with which men can credit themselves." "We should value life," he declares, "as a field of action." We should care for the doing of things quite as much as for the results. Tried by this standard, aspiration and effort are to be more highly prized than achievement itself. The man who sincerely strives for a great object has succeeded, whether or not the object is attained or its attainment brings any tangible reward.

It is no novelty, of course, to hear a college president upholding ideal standards and rejecting utilitarian views of success, but few of the educators have cared to follow their theories, as President Hadley does, to their logical conclusion. Probably a majority of them would applaud Nansen's courage in attempting to reach the north pole but would question the utility of the attempt. President Hadley admires Nansen simply "because he succeeded in getting so much nearer the pole than anybody before him ever did," and thinks it is one of the most discouraging testimonies to the false standards of the nineteenth century that Nansen feels compelled to justify himself on the basis of the scientific results of his expedition. Furthermore, a man who tries to get to the pole is engaged in a glorious play, "which justifies more risk and more expenditure of life than would be warranted for a few miserable entomological specimens, however remote from the place where they had previously been found."

The young man of to-day has no lack of exhortations to lead the life of strenuous effort. It is as well that he should be taught also that the reward for this effort will be barren if the whole object sought be material benefit to himself. Life is something to be used. Whether or not it has been successfully used depends not on the results so much as on the object sought and the earnestness of the seeking. It is somewhat novel to find an American college president expounding this philosophy to his students, but the philosophy is, on the whole, helpful. It will spur to effort in crises where the desire for more material success fails to provide a sufficient incentive.

A certain New York author is fond of his own work, and Robert W. Chambers is responsible for the story that he called at one of the libraries to find out how his latest book was going. He hoped to have his vanity tickled a little.

"Is———————in?" he said to the librarian, naming his book.

"It never was out," was the reply.

What is a great love of books? It is something like a personal introduction to the great and good men of all past times. Books, it is true, are silent as you see them on your shelves; but, silent as they are, when I enter a library I feel almost as if the dead were present, and I know if I put questions to these books they will answer me with all the faithfulness and fullness which has been left in them by the great men who have left the books with us.—*John Bright.*

The spring poet has been much exploited in the comic papers. The would-be novelist has been plastered with signs and tokens until one could not fail to recognize him in the dark. But the ordinary, commonplace, experienced writer has been so shamefully neglected that few realize his virtues. The editor recognizes his manuscript as far off as he can see it, and seizes upon it with joy. The manuscript is typewritten and punctuated. It bears the author's name and address at the top of the first page. It is signed with the author's name at the end. It is NOT tied with a blue ribbon. No, the blue ribbon habit is not a myth. It really exists in every form from pale baby to navy No. 4 and in every shape from a hard knot to an elaborate rosette.—*Munsey's.*

XX.
THE LENGTHENING
LIST OF PATRONS

During the year 1906 the patrons of the Fiction Factory steadily increased in number. *The Blue Book, The Red Book, The Railroad Man's, The All-Story, The People's*—all these magazines bought of the Factory's products, some of them very liberally. The old patrons, also, were retained, Harte & Perkins taking a supply of nickel novels and a Stella Edwards' serial for *The Guest.*

Edwards' introduction to *The Blue Book* came so late in the year that the business falls properly within the affairs of 1907. The first step, however, was taken on Aug. 13, 1906, and was in the form of the following letter:

"My dear Mr. Edwards:

Why don't you send me, with a view to publication in *The Blue Book,* as we have renamed our old *Monthly Story Magazine,* one or more of those weird and fantastic novelettes of yours? If you have anything ready, let me see it. I can at least assure you of a prompt decision and equally prompt payment if the story goes. Anything you may have up to 6,000 words I shall be very glad to see for *The Red Book.*

Yours very truly,
"Karl Edwin Harriman."

Here was a pleasant surprise for Edwards. He had met Mr. Harriman the year before in Battle Creek, Michigan. At that time Mr. Harriman was busily engaged hiding his talents under a bushel known as *The Pilgrim Magazine.* When the Red Book Corporation of Chicago, kicked the basket to one side, grabbed Mr. Harriman out from under it and made off with him, the aspect of the heavens promised great things for literature in the Middle West. And this promise, by the way, is being splendidly fulfilled.

When you take down your "Who's Who" to look up some personage sufficiently notorious to have a place between its red covers, if you find at the end of his name the words, "editor, author," you may be sure that there is no cloud on the title that gives him a place in the book. You will know at once that he must have been a good author or he would never have been promoted from the ranks; and having been a good author he is certainly a better editor than if the case were otherwise, for he knows both ends of the publishing trade.

Having been through the mill himself, Mr. Harriman has a fellow-feeling for his contributors. He knows what it is to take a lay figure for a plot, clothe it in suitable language, cap it with a climax and put it on exhibition with a card: "Here's a Peach! Grab me quick for $9.99." Harriman's "peaches" never came back. The author of "Ann Arbor Tales," "The Girl and the Deal," and others has been successful right from the start.

No request for material received at the Edwards' Factory ever fails of a prompt and hearty response. A short story and a novelette were at once put on the stocks. They were constructed slowly, for Edwards could give them attention only during odd moments taken from his regular work. The short story was finished and submitted long in advance of the novelette. This letter, dated Sept. 18, will show its success:

"My Dear Old Man: Why don't you run on here and see me, now and again. Oh, yes, New York's a lot better, but we're doing things here, too. About 'Cast Away by Contract,' it's very funny—such a ridiculously absurd idea that it's quite irresistible. How will $75 be for it? O. K.? It's really all I can afford to pay for a story of its sort, and I do want you in the book. Let me hear as soon as possible and I will give it out to the artist.

Very truly yours,
"K. H."

And so began the business with Mr. Harriman. He still, at this writing (1911), has a running account on the Factory's books and is held in highest esteem by the proprietor.

A letter, written May 13, 1905, (a year dealt with in a previous chapter), is reproduced here as having a weighty bearing on the events of 1906. It was Edwards' first letter from a gentleman who had recently allied himself with the Munsey publications. As a publisher Mr. F. A. Munsey is conceded to be a star of the first magnitude, but this genius is manifest in nothing so much as in his ability to surround himself with men capable of pushing his ideas to their highest achievement. Such a man had been added to his editorial staff in the person of Mr. R. H. Davis. Mr. Davis, like Mr. Bryan, hails originally from Nebraska. Although he differs somewhat from Mr. Bryan in political views, he has the same powers as a spellbinder. He's Western, all through, is "Bob" Davis, bluff, hearty and equally endowed with stories, snap and sincerity.

"Dear Sir:

We would like to have a few pictures of those writers who have contributed considerably to our various magazines. It is obvious that this refers to you. Therefore, if you will send us a portrait it will be greatly appreciated.

Very truly yours,
"R. H. Davis."

Mr. Davis got the picture; also a serial or two and some short stories for new publications issued by the Munsey Company of which he was editor. Late in 1905 he called for a railroad serial, and he wanted a particularly good one.

Edwards had never tried his hand at such a story. He knew, in a general way, that the "pilot" was on the front end of a locomotive, and that the "tender" was somewhere in the rear, but his technical knowledge was hazy and unreliable. The story, if accepted, was to appear in *The Railroad Man's Magazine,* would be read by "railroaders" the country over, and would be damned and laughed at if it contained any technical "breaks."

Here was just the sort of a nut Edwards liked to crack. The perils of the undertaking lent it a zest, and were a distinct aid to industry and inspiration. He resolved that he would give Mr. Davis a story that would bear the closest scrutiny of railroad men and win their interest and applause. To this end he studied railroads, up and down and across. He absorbed what he could from books, and the rest he secured through personal investigation. When the story was done, he submitted the manuscript to a veteran of the rails—one who had been both a telegraph operator and engineer—and this gentleman had not a change to suggest! Mr. Davis took the story aboard. While it was running in the magazine a reader wrote in to declare that it must have been written by an old hand at the railroad game: the author of the letter had been railroading for thirty-five years himself, and felt positive that he ought to know! "The Red Light at Rawlines" scored a triumph, proving the value of study, and the ability to adjust one's self to an untried situation.

Edwards had imbibed too much technical knowledge to exhaust it all on one story, so he wrote another and sent it to Mr. White. The latter informed him:

"I turned 'Special One-Five-Three' over to *The Railroad Man's Magazine* at once, without reading it, and they are sending you a check for it this week, I understand. This does not mean that I did not care to consider it for *The Argosy*. I certainly have an opening for more of your stories, but when you took the railroad for your theme and treated it so intelligently, I think it better that you give *The Argosy* some other subject matter."

Another story, written this year to order, also serves to show that facility in handling strange themes or environments does not always depend upon personal acquaintance with the subject in hand. Intelligent study and investigation can many times, if not always, piece out a lack of personal experience. Blazing a course through *terra incognita* in such a manner, however, is not without its dangers.

Harte & Perkins wished to begin the yearly volume of *The Guest* with a Stella Edwards serial. This story was to have, for its background, the San Francisco earthquake. Nearly the whole action of the yarn was to take place in the city itself. Edwards had never been there. He had vague ideas regarding the "Golden Gate," Oakland and other places, but for accurate knowledge he was as much at sea as in the case of the railroad story. He set the wheels of industry to revolving, however, and familiarized himself so thoroughly with the city from books, newspapers and magazines that the editor of *The Guest,* an old San Francisco newspaper man, had this to say about the story:

"It will please you to learn that we think 'A Romance of the Earthquake' a very interesting story, with plenty of brisk action, picturesque in description, and DISPLAYING A THOROUGH KNOWLEDGE OF CALIFORNIA'S METROPOLIS AND VICINITY."

Although these are interesting problems to solve, yet Edwards, as a rule, prefers dealing with material that has formed a part of his own personal experiences.

His "prospecting" trip for the year brought him into New York on Monday, Nov. 12. On Tuesday (his "lucky day," according to the Coney Island seer of fateful memory), he called on Mr. White, and Mr. White took him across the hall and introduced him to Mr. Davis. The latter gentleman ordered four serials and, for stories of a certain length, agreed to pay $500 each.

Next day Edwards dropped in at the offices of Street & Smith and submitted a novelette—"The Billionaire's Dilemma"—to Mr. MacLean, editor of *The Popular Magazine* (Mr. Lewis having retired from that publication some time before). Mr. MacLean carried the manuscript in to Mr. Vivian M. Moses, editor of *People's,* and the latter bought it. This story made a hit in the *People's* and won from Mr. George C. Smith, of the firm, a personal letter of commendation. Result: More work for *The People's Magazine.*

About the middle of December, Edwards and his wife left for their home in Michigan. They had been in the city a month, and during that time Edwards had received $1150 for his Factory's products. The year, financially, was the best Edwards had so far experienced; but it was to be outdone by the year that followed.

During 1907 a great deal of writing was done for Mr. Davis. Among other stories submitted to him was

one which Edwards called, "On the Stroke of Four."
Regarding it Mr. Davis had expressed himself, May 6,
in characteristic vein:

"My dear Colonel:
  Send it along. The title is not a bad one. I suppose it
will arrive at a quarter past five, as you are generally late....
  Now that spring is here, go out and chop a few kindlings
against the canning of the fruit. This season we are going to
preserve every dam thing on the farm. In the meantime, put
up a few bartletts for little Willie. We may drop in provided
the nest contains room."

He received an urgent invitation to "drop in." But
he didn't. He backed out. Possibly he was afraid he
would have to "pioneer it" in the country, after years
of metropolitan luxury in the effete East. Or perhaps
he was afraid that Edwards might read some
manuscripts to him. Whatever the cause, he never appeared to claim the "bartletts," made ready for him with
so much painstaking care by Mrs. Edwards. But this
was not the only count in the indictment. He sent back
"On the Stroke of Four!" And this was his message:

  "Up to page 106 this story is a peach. After that it is a
peach, but a rotten peach, and I'd be glad to have you fix it
up and return it."

After Edwards has finished a story he has an in-
grained dislike for tampering with it any further. However, had he not been head over ears in other work, he
would probably have "fixed up" the manuscript for
Mr. Davis. In the circumstances, he decided to try its
fortunes elsewhere. Mr. Moses took it in, paid $400
for it, and pronounced it better than "The Billionaire's
Dilemma."

At a later date, Mr. Davis wanted another sea story
for *Ocean* which, at that time, was surging considerably. "On the Stroke of Four" had been designed to

fill such an order. Inasmuch as it had failed, Edwards wrote a second yarn which was accepted at $450.

The sea, and the people who go down to it in ships, to say nothing of the ships themselves, were all out of Edwards' usual line. He prepared himself by reading every sea story he could lay hands on, long or short. He bought text-books on seamanship and navigation, and whenever there were manoeuvers connected with "working ship" in a story, Edwards puzzled them out with the help of the text-books. With both deep-water serials he succeeded tolerably well. He is sure, at least, that he didn't get the spanker-boom on the foremast, nor the jib too far aft.

Harte & Perkins again favored the Factory with an order for a "Stella Edwards" to begin another volume of *The Guest*. This was an automobile story, "The Hero of the Car," and was accepted and highly praised.

Another novelette, "An Aerial Romance," was bought by Mr. Moses for *The People's Magazine*.

Beginning in March, Edwards had written some more nickel novels for Harte & Perkins—not the old Five-Cent Weekly, for that he was never to do again—but various stories, in odd lots, to help out with a particular series. On July 14 he was switched to another line of half-dime fiction, and this work he kept throughout the remainder of the year.

For the two years the Factory's showing stands as follows:

1906:
18 nickel novels @ $50 each..........................$ 900.00
Royalties on book, Dillingham........................   10.20
"The World's Wonder," 300.00
"A Romance of the Earthquake," 250.00
"The Sheriff Who Lost and Won," 300.00

"The Reporter's Scoop," 60.00
"The Deputy Sheriff," 40.00
"The Red Light at Rawlin's," 350.00
"Cast Away by Contract," 75.00
"Special One-Five-Three," 350.00
"The Disputed Claim," 500.00
"Fencing with Foes," 450.00
"The Billionaire's Dilemma," 200.00

Total. ....·.......... ....$3785.20

1907:
"Under Sealed Orders," ....$ 250.00
"The Pacific Pearlers," 450.00
"Call of the West," 200.00
"Wilderness Gold-Hunter," 500.00
"Dupes of Destiny," 75.00
"On the Stroke of Four," 400.00
"The Hero of the Car," 300.00
"An Aerial Romance," 200.00
"West-Indies Mix-Up," 60.00
33 nickel novels @ $50 each 1650.00

Total. ....·................. ....$4085.00

In that remarkable group of authors who made the dime novel famous, the late Col. Prentiss Ingraham was one of the giants. These "ready writers" thought nothing of turning out a thousand words of original matter in an hour, in the days when the click of the typewriter was unknown, and of keeping it up until a novel of 70,000 words was easily finished in a week. But to Col. Ingraham belongs the unique distinction of having composed and written out a complete story of 35,000 words with a fountain pen, between breakfast and breakfast. His equipment as a writer of stories for boys was most varied and valuable, garnered from his experience as an officer in the Confederate army, his service both on shore and sea in the Cuban war for independence, and in travels in Mexico, Austria, Greece and Africa. But he is best known and will be most loyally remembered for his Buffalo Bill tales, the number of which he himself scarcely knew, and which possessed peculiar value from his intimate personal friendship with Col. Cody.

XXI.

A WRITER'S
READING

That old Egyptian who put above the door of his
library these words, "Books are the Medicines of the
Soul," was wise indeed. But the Wise, ever since books
have been made, have harped on the advantage of good
literature, and have said all there is to be said on the
subject a thousand times over. If one has any doubts
on this point let him consult a dictionary of quotations.
No intelligent person disputes the value of books; and
it should be self-evident that no writer, whose business
is the making of books, will do so. To the writer books
are not only "medicines for the soul" but tonics for his
technique, febrifuges for his rhetorical fevers and pro-
phylactics for the thousand and one ills that beset his
calling. A wide course of general reading—the wider
the better—is part of the fictionist's necessary equipment; and of even more importance is a specializing
along the lines of his craft.

"Omniverous reader" is an overworked term, but it
is perfect in its application to Edwards. From his youth
up he has devoured everything in the way of books
he could lay his hands on. The volumes came hap-haz-
ard, and the reading has been desultory and, for the most
part, without system. If engaged on a railroad story,
he reads railroad stories; if a tale of the sea claims his
attention, then his pabulum consists of sea-facts and fiction, and so on. The latest novel is a passion with him,

and he would rather read a story by Jack London, or Rex Beach, or W. J. Locke than eat or sleep—or write something more humble although his very own. He is fond of history, too, and among the essayists he loves his Emerson. Nothing so puts his modest talents in a glow as to bring them near the beacon lights of Genius.

Edwards has a library of goodly proportions, but it is a hodge-podge of everything under the sun. Thomas Carlyle "keeps company" with Mary Johnston on his bookshelves, Marcus Aurelius rubs elbows with Frank Spearman, "France in the Nineteenth Century" nestles close to "The Mystery" from the firm of White & Adams, and four volumes of Thackeray are cheek by jowl with Harland's "The Cardinal's Snuff-Box." A most reprehensible method of book keeping, of course, but to Edwards' it is a delightful confusion. To him the method is reprehensible only when he wants a certain book and has to spend half a day looking for it. Some time, some blessed time—he has promised himself for years and years,—he will catalogue his books just as he has catalogued his clippings.

Books that concern themselves with the writer's trade are many, so many that they may be termed literally an embarrassment of riches. If a writer had them all he would have more than he needed or could use. Books on the short story by J. Berg Eisenwein and James Knapp Reeve, Edwards considers indispensable. They are to be read many times and thoroughly mastered. "Roget's Thesaurus" is a work which Edwards' consulted until it was dogeared and coverless; he then presented it to an impecunious friend with a well-defined case of *writeritis* and has since contented himself with the large "Thesaurus Dictionary of the English Language," by F. A. March, LL. D. This flanks him on the left, as he sits at his typewriter, while Webster's "Unabridged" closes him in on the right. The Standard Dictionary is also within reach. Dozens and dozens of books about writers and writing have been read and are now gathering dust. After a writer has once charged himself to the brim with "technique," he should cease to bother about it. If he has read to some purpose his work will be as near technical perfection as is necessary, for unconsciously he will follow the canons of the art; while if he loads and fires these "canons" too often, they will be quite apt to burst and blow him into that innocuous desuetude best described as "mechanical." He should exercise all the freedom possible within legitimate bounds, and so acquire individuality and "style"—whatever that is.

No sane man in any line of trade or manufacturing will attempt to do business without subscribing to one or more papers or magazines covering his particular field. He wants the newest labor-saving wrinkle, the latest discoveries, tips on new markets, facts as to what others in the same business are doing, and countless other fresh and pertinent items which a good trade paper will furnish. A writer is such a man, and he needs tabulated facts as much as any other tradesman or manufacturer. Periodicals dealing with the trade of authorship are few, but they are helpful to a degree which it is difficult to estimate.

From the beginning of his work Edwards has made it a point to acquire every publication that dealt with the business of his Fiction Factory. In early years he had *The Writer,* and then *The Author.* When these went the way of good but unprofitable things, THE EDITOR fortunately happened along, and proved incomparably better in every detail.

From its initial number THE EDITOR has been a monthly guest at the Factory, always cordially welcomed and given a place of honor. Guide, counsellor and friend—it has proved to be all these.

Edwards subscribes heartily to that benevolent policy known as "the helping hand." Furthermore, he tries to live up to it. What little success he has had with his Fiction Factory he has won by his own unaided efforts; but there were times, along at the beginning, when he could have avoided disappointment and useless labor if some one who knew had advised him. Realizing what "the helping hand" might have done in his own case, he has always felt the call to extend it to others. Assistance is useless, however, if a would-be writer hasn't something to say and doesn't know how to say it. Another who has had some success may secure the novice a considerate hearing, but from that on the matter lies wholly with the novice himself. If he has it in him, he will win; if he hasn't, he will fail. Edwards first advice to those who have sought his help has invariably been this: "Subscribe to THE EDITOR." In nearly every instance the advice has been taken, and with profitable results.

This same advice is given here, should the reader stand in need of a proper start along the thorny path of authorship. Nor is it to be construed in any manner as an advertisement. It is merely rendering justice where justice is due, and is an honest tribute to a publication for writers, drawn from an experience of twenty-two years "in the ranks."

XXII.

NEW SOURCES
OF PROFIT

The out-put of the Fiction Factory brought excellent returns during the years 1908 and 1909. Industry followed close on the heels of opportunity and the result was more than gratifying. The 1908 product consisted of forty-four nickel novels for Harte & Perkins, two novelettes for *The Blue Book,* four serials for the Munsey publications, and one novelette for *The People's Magazine.* This work alone would have carried the receipts well above those of the preceding year, but new and unexpected sources of profit helped to enlarge the showing on the Factory's books.

The rapidity with which Edwards wrote his serial stories—sometimes under the spur of an immediate demand from his publishers, and sometimes under the less relentless spur of personal necessity—seemed to preclude the possibility of profit on a later publication "in cloth." Only a finished performance is worthy of a durable binding. Realizing this, Edwards had never made a determined effort to interest book-publishers in the stories. In the ordinary course of affairs, and with scarcely any attention on his part, two serials found their way into "cloth." "Danny W.," accepted and brought out by Dodd, Mead & Co., was written for book publication, and serialized after it had appeared in that form. It fell as far short of a "best seller" as did the two republished serials.

Nevertheless, in spite of the fact that additional profit through publication in cloth seemed out of the question, Edwards wondered if there were not something else to be gained from the stories besides the serial rights.

His stories were dramatic and, in several instances, had appealed to play-writers. For a time he had hopes that dramatic rights might prove a source of additional income. His hopes, in this respect, have not been completely dashed, inasmuch as competent hands are at this date (September, 1911) fitting some of his stories for the stage. Something may come of it, but his experience has made him wary and he is not at all sanguine.

Eliminating book and dramatic rights from the equation, and what remained? A letter from Waltham, Mass., dated April 23, 1908, uncovered possibilities of which Edwards had never dreamed. Most of these possibilities, as it transpired, *were* a dream, but, as in the matter of dramatic rights, some day the dream may come true in a large and substantial manner. Here is the letter:

"Dear Sir:

If you have not yet disposed of the sole and unrestricted rights of translation into the GERMAN language of your books: 'The Billionaire's Dilemma' and 'The Shadow of the Unknown,' will you permit me to submit them to my GERMAN correspondents—some of the best known GERMAN PUBLISHERS —with the idea of effecting a sale?

I shall require a single copy of 'The Billionaire's Dilema,' but not of 'The Shadow of the Unknown' having preserved the story as it appeared first in the POPULAR,* to send abroad, with a statement of the best terms you will make for the *cash out-right purchase of both book and serial rights.*

If the serial rights of translation in GERMAN belong to the POPULAR, you will have to come to a satisfactory understanding with them, in order to legally assign to me the SERIAL, as well as your own individual, book-rights, because all GERMAN publishers insist on serial rights, although they

*A mistake, the story appeared in **The Blue Book.**

seldom or never use them, as MAGAZINES are not good and little used there.

My experience has been, that the MAGAZINE COMPAN-IES are very broad in their treatment of their writers, and usually willing to re-transfer their SERIAL rights of transla-tion, in order to facilitate a sale, and make them universally known.

Of course less is paid for translation rights of stories that have only appeared in SERIAL form in the STATES.

If any of the publishers I represent purchases your stories, you have the best possible guarantee of perfect translation and speedy publication.

Awaiting the courtesy of an early reply and the necessary copy of 'The Billionaire's Dilemma,' I have the honor to be, dear Sir, Yours very truly,

"Eugene Niemann."*

Several guns were fired during this invasion of Germany, but only one shell "went home." This was not the fault of Mr. Niemann. In Edwards' brief experience with him he found him always a scholar and a gentleman. Sincerity and courtesy were his never-failing traits. The pleasant little twists he gave his English, and the occasional naive expression that struggled through his typewriter, along with the prodigal use of "caps," will perhaps excuse a further offering from the correspondence. Here is the shot that hit the mark:

"May 12, 1908.

"Dear Sir:—

Before I have even had time to forward 'The Billionaire's Dilemma' and 'On the Stroke of Four', and to await your other announced stories, a letter comes from one of my German cor-respondents, saying he had run through your short story: "The Shadow of the Unknown' and would purchase the rights of translation if you will accept an offer of FORTY DOLLARS.

Perhaps you will say, "such an offer is absurd," but first let me state to you, that the best books placed in GERMANY bring at the most ONE HUNDRED DOLLARS, and oftener anywhere from FIFTY to ONE HUNDRED, that the chief

*Edwards uses a ficticious name for this correspondent.

profit, is not a monetary one, rather the spreading of the writer's name and fame.

"The Shadow of the Unknown,' writes the publisher, is a very short story, and if you will be guided by my long experience, dear Sir, you will accept the offer, in order to make our name popular and facilitate a better sale of your following stories, which I shall take double pleasure in forwarding, feeling surer of a good offer.

Were I guilty of business indiscretion, you would be surprised to know the names of the already published 'BOOKS' I have sold and am daily selling the GERMAN rights of, for hardly a monetary consideration at all, and yet the literary satisfaction quite out-balances all other considerations, does it not?

I enclose the customary form of assignment, which you can sign and have duly witnessed by a NOTARY PUBLIC, if you see fit to accept the offer, and which you will please then send me per AMERICAN EXPRESS C. O. D. subject to examination to avoid every possible chance of error.

The personal receipt need not be signed before the NOTARY PUBLIC, your signature without witness suffices.

Hoping to do much better for you with your other fine stories and appreciating your confidence, I remain, dear Sir,

Very truly yours,

"EUGENE NIEMANN."

After the dust had settled, and the invasion was finally completed, $40 had been added to the year's receipts of the Fiction Factory; but Edwards clings to the hope that some day more of his "fine stories" may be greedily bought by the German publishers. These German publishers are honorable enough to buy, where they might pirate, and there are a few American publishers who might take lessons from them in business probity. With a small tidbit from a letter of May 18, the pleasant Mr. Niemann will be dismissed:

"Later, with your permission, I will take up the stories I sell in GERMANY for sale in FRANCE, DENMARK, NORWAY and SWEDEN?

The monetary remuneration in the SCANDINAVIAN countries is yet smaller than in GERMANY, but the people are fine readers, and that for all, who truly LOVE their ART is the chief standpoint I take it?!"

During the latter part of July and the earlier part of August Edwards was in New York for a couple of weeks. As usual when in the city he worked even harder than he did at home. Two nickel novels were written, a serial was put through the Factory for Mr. Davis, and he collected $200 for a novelette which he sold to *People's*. There was an interesting, almost a humorous, circumstance connected with the serial.

Edwards called the story "The Man Who Left." When the manuscript was completed he took it in to Mr. Davis, and two or three days later called again to learn its fate.

The Munsey offices are up close to the roof in the Flatiron building. The lair of the editor who presides over the destinies of *The All-Story Magazine, The Railroad Man's Magazine* and *The Scrap Book** is flanked on one side by a prospect of space that causes the occasional caller to hang on to his chair. Across from this dizzy void is a partition hung with framed photographs of contributors—a rogues' gallery in which Edwards, when he last saw the collection, had a prominent place. North of an imaginary line drawn between the window and the partition sits the editor, grimly prominent against a motto-covered wall. As the caller faces the editor he is, of course, confronted by placards reminding him that "This is My Busy Day—Cut it Short," and "Find A Man for the Job not A Job for the Man," and others cunningly calculated to put him on tenterhooks.

To this place, therefore, came Edwards, proffering inquiries about "The Man Who Left." He read fateful things in the august countenance, and he was not sur-

*Now no more as **The Cavalier,** the former monthly, now a weekly has "absorbed" **The Scrap Book.**

prised when Mr. Davis handed him a lemon, but he *was* surprised when he took the lemon back.

"Rotten," said Mr. Davis, "r-r-rotten! When I'm out for peaches, Edwards, I side-step the under-ripe persimmons. 'The Man Who Left' ought to have made his get-away along about line one, paragraph one, chapter one; and then if he had staid out plumb to the place where you have written 'Finis' this gorgeous but unconvincing tale would have been vastly improved. Am I a Jasper that you seek thus to inveigle me into purchasing a gold-brick? Here, take it away! Now let me have it again. I am going to give you three hundred for it and tuck it away in the strong-box. Later you are to evolve, write and otherwise put upon paper a fictional prize for which 'The Man Who Left' will be returned to you in even exchange. Do you get me? 'Nuff said. I think you're out of mazuma, and that's why I'm doing this. My friends'll ruin me yet!"

Now the humor, if there is any, fits in about here: Edwards went back to Michigan and wrote a serial which he sent on to replace "The Man Who Left." Here is the letter in reply:

My dear Edwards:

While I was away on my vacation, some one spilled a pitcher of milk. In other words, they put "The Man Who Left" to press for *The All-Story Magazine,* and it is now too late to yank it back. That's the trouble of leaving anything in the safe that should not be there. You and I, however, being practical men, can understand the facility with which the yarn was nabbed up.

Now, the point is, I can use the "Mydus" yarn and get a check off to you next week, provided I have some basis on which to operate. What's the lowest price for which you will give me 'Mydus,' call all previous arrangements equal, and let things stand as they are. The way to trim me and square accounts is to come back with a quick, short, sharp, cheap reply, and let it go at that.

Hurry up this 'Mydus' business and we'll see what we can do. Sincerely yours,

"R. H. DAVIS."

The spilling of that "pitcher of milk" while Mr. Davis was away on his vacation had netted Edwards just an even $300.

Another source of profit from the serial stories which the Fiction Factory had been turning out for years was revealed to Edwards in a letter dated Nov. 19, 1908. This, like the matter of translation rights, came to Edwards as a pleasant surprise; but, unlike the "German invasion," it was to prove vastly more profitable. Here is the letter:

"Dear Sir:

Upon looking over the files of *The Argosy* we find that you have written the following serial stories. Are the book rights of these your property? If not, can you get Mr. Munsey to give them to you? If you can, and will lengthen the stories to about 75,000 words, we will pay you $100 each for the paper book rights of same.

We cannot offer you more, as we would put these out in cheap paper edition, but this publication would do a great deal toward popularizing your name and work with the class of readers who buy *The Argosy* and other fiction magazines.

The stories are as follows: (Here were listed the titles of seven *Argosy* serials.) Very truly yours,

"STREET & SMITH."

Edwards caught at this opportunity. He failed to realize, at the time, just how much work was involved in lengthening the stories for paper-book publication. In his reply to Street & Smith he offered a list of forty-five serials, and promised others if they could use so many. He was requested, on Dec. 4, to forward copies of all the stories for reading. The same letter contained this paragraph:

"I note that your letter is dated December 2nd and that you state you expect to be in New York inside of three weeks. I think it might be to our mutual advantage if you could come on in a week or ten days, for there is a new line of work which I think you could do for us about which I would like to talk with you."

Just before Christmas Edwards and his wife arrived in New York. On some of the serials which had appeared in the Munsey magazines Edwards owned all but serial rights, but there were many more wherein all rights were held by the publishers.

The folly of a writer's selling all rights when disposing of a story for serial publication dawned upon Edwards very strongly, at this time. The conviction was driven "home" at a little dinner which Edwards tendered to several editors and readers. During the course of the dinner one of the guests—an editor in charge of a prominent and popular magazine—averred bluntly that "any writer who sells all rights to a story to a magazine using the story serially, is a fool."

With Edwards this sale of all rights had resulted from carelessness more than anything else, and had he not been dealing with friends like Mr. White and Mr. Davis he might have suffered financial loss because of his folly. Two or three interviews with Mr. Davis secured the paper-book rights, but with the understanding that if any of the lengthened stories were brought out in cloth, one-half of the royalties were to go to The Munsey Company.

In the whole list there were only seven stories long enough for immediate issue in paper-book form. These were paid for, at once. The other stories fell short of the required number of words all the way from 5,000 to 30,000 words. There was no profit to Edwards in lengthening the stories at the price of $100 each. What benefit he derived—and is now deriving, for the work continues—was in the advertising which the wide circulation of the paper-covered books afforded him. Also, Edwards considered the value of cementing his friendship with the old-established publishing house of Street & Smith, a house noted for the fairness of its dealings with contributors and for the prompt payment for all material upon acceptance. "Making good" with publishers of such high standing is always of inestimable value to a writer.

One of Street & Smith's editors, at this time, was St. George Rathborne, author of "Dr. Jack" and dozens of other popular stories that have appeared in paper covers. Here was another author who had become an editor, bringing to his duties an experience and ability that made for the highest success. Mr. C. A. MacLean, another member of the Street & Smith editorial staff, was also a gentleman with whom Edwards had occasional dealings. Mr. MacLean, beginning at the lowest rung of the ladder, had mounted steadily to the post of editor of *The Popular Magazine* and *Smith's Magazine,* by sheer force of his own merit pushing those publications to the forefront of magazines of their class. To these gentlemen, and particularly to Mr. Rathborne,* Edwards is indebted for unfailing kindness and courtesy, and takes this means to acknowledge it.

*Mr. Rathborne has recently given up his editorial duties and has retired to what seems to be the ultimate goal of writers and editors—a farm. He is somewhere in New Jersey.

The special work which was mentioned in Street & Smith's letter of Nov. 19 consisted of a new weekly publication for which Edwards was to furnish the copy. Seventy-five dollars each was to be paid for these stories.

With all this work ahead of the Fiction Factory, the year 1909 dawned in a blaze of prosperity. During 1909 Edwards found himself so busy with the paper-books and the other publication that he had no time for serial stories. After thirty-four issues the new publication was discontinued, and Edwards went back to writing novels for Harte & Perkins, at $60 each.

During 1909 Edwards tried his hand at moving pictures. The alluring advertisements under the scare-head, "We Pay $10 to $100 for Picture Plays," caught his eye and fired his ambition. He wrote a scenario, sent it in, and waited expectantly for his $100. He had been only two hours preparing the ".photoplay" and it looked like "easy money." When the check arrived it was for $10! He wrote in to ask what had become of the remaining $90? Thus answered The Vitagraph Company of America, Oct. 27, '09:

"In regard to the payment for a manuscript of this character, we never give more than ten dollars, for two or three reasons.

In the first place, we only use the idea. The manuscript has to be revised in almost every instance in order to put it in practical shape for the directors.

Again, they contain an idea which is more or less stereotyped or conventional and cannot be claimed as entirely original only as applied to the action of the play.

Regarding your own idea, I will frankly say that the same idea has often been embodied in other plays, but the general suggestion of it gives a new phase to the action of the idea.

THE EDITOR merely surmises, or so we think, that a thoroughly original manuscript in practical shape would be

worth at least $25, but we seldom get one of that kind.   We
would welcome one at any time and would pay its full value.

The members of our staff, who are obliged to write practical
working scenarios, appreciate the above facts because they know
what it means to perfect a scenario with the synopsis of the
story, the properties, settings, &c., &c.

We merely state these things so you will understand that we
are thoroughly fair in your case and will certainly be so in
every instance.

Ideas, if they are entirely original, would be worth more
than ten dollars, but they are scarcer than hen's teeth at any
price.

We find most of the ideas which we receive, and we receive
hundreds of them, are nothing but repetition or old ones in new
guises.

Again we will say, if we can get original ideas we will pay
their full value."

Another case of *sic transit*—this time, *sic transit
mazuma*.

Here follows a transcript from the Factory's books
for the two years with which this chapter has dealt:

1908:

Dillingham, last royalties on "Tales of Two Towns"..$	1.50
45 nickel novels @ $50 each........................	2250.
"The Shadow of the Unknown".....................	200.
"The Shadow of the Unknown," translation rights....	40.
"Parker & O'Fallon".............................	300.
"In the Valley's Shadow"..........................	200.
"The Man Who Left,".............................	300.
"Trail of the Mydus,".............................	350.
"Just A Dollar,".................................	350.
"Frisbie's Folly,"................................	350.
"The Man Called Dare,"...........................	300.
"The Streak of Yellow,"..........................	200.
7 paper-book rights at $100 each, ...	700.
Total, ...	$5541.50

1909:

34 issues "Motor Boys" @ $75 each ....$	2550.
21 paper-book rights @ $100 each	2100.
9 nickel novels @ $60 each,.......................	540.
"The Stop on the 'Scutcheon," short story	35.

THE FICTION FACTORY

Moving-picture, ... 10.
"Breaking Even," short story .... 40.
"Divided by Eight," short story .... 35.

Total ....·............ ......$ 5310.

The following advertisement from an English paper,
which is vouched for, once more illustrates the truth of
the statement that fact is stranger than fiction. The
owner of the houses, it may be mentioned, was ill in
bed, far away, and the neighbors evidently did not question the right of the men to do as they did. The
advertisement is as follows:

LOST.—Three fine cottages have mysteriously dis-
appeared from the property Nos. 296, 298 and 300 High
road, Willesden Green, London.   Please communicate
with J. M. Godwin, 71 Bank Street, London, W. C.

O. Henry told a whimsical tale of what he considered
unfair competition in the short story field. He was in
the office of a big magazine, when he witnessed the return to a dejected looking young fellow of a couple of
manuscripts. "I am sorry for that fellow," said the
editor. "He came to New York from New Orleans a
year ago, and regularly brings some stories to our
office. We can never use them. He doesn't make a dollar by his pen, and he is getting shabby and pale."
A month or so later O. Henry saw the same writer in
the same office, and the editor was talking to him
earnestly. "You had better go back to New Orleans,"
said that gentleman.   "Why?" said the young man.
"Some day I may write a story you may want." "But
you can do that just as well in New Orleans," said the
editor, "and you can save board bills." "Board bills,"
ejaculated the young man. "What do I care about
board bills! I have an income of twenty thousand a
year from my father's estate."

157

XXIII.

THE INJUSTICE
OF IT

The commercial world may hearken sentimentally to that plaintive ballad, "Silver Threads Among the Gold," as it floats into the Emporium from a street organ, but the commercial world never allows sentiment to interfere with business. When a man presents himself and asks for a job, he is examined for symptoms of decrepitude before his mental abilities are canvassed. The wise seeker for place, before making the rounds of the Want Column, will see to it that his hair is of a youthful color, for there is nothing so damned by the octopus of trade as hoary locks. A bottle of walnut juice, carefully administered, may bridge the gap and lead from failure to success.

"New blood!" that's the cry. "Age is too conservative, too partial to the old and outworn standards, too apt to keep in a rut. Give us the mop of black hair and the bright, snappy eye! Give us energy and brilliant daring and a fresh view-point! We'll be taking a few chances, but what of that? We must follow the fashion."

Some of the publishers have gone to the extreme of the prevailing mode. The yearling from the football field, if he happens to have been sporting editor of the college journal, is brought to the sanctum, shoved into the chair of authority, and given $50 a week and the power to go ahead and be ruthless. He rarely disappoints his employer. Whenever he does, his employer is to be congratulated. Usually, however, he sticks to his schedule. He thinks he is Somebody, and attempts to prove it by kicking all the old contributors out of the office and forwarding invitations for manuscripts to every member of the Class of '10.

There is no writer of experience who has failed to meet this sort of editor. For years a publishing house may have steadily increased in power and prestige through the loyalty and labor of the old contributor, only to give some darling of the campus a desk and the authority to begin oslerizing faithfulness and ability.

This injustice would be humorous were some of its aspects not so tragic. The smug publishers themselves may have something to answer for. They have wrung their ratings in Dun and Bradstreet from the old contributor, and when they abandon a policy that has brought success they are steering through troubled waters and into unknown seas.

For anything short of incompetence this casting aside of the old in order to try out the new is reprehensible. To weather a decade or two of storm and stress a writer must have been versatile. Versatility increases with his years, and he is as capable of brilliant daring and a fresh viewpoint as any youth in the twenties.

Times out of number this has been made manifest. Stories disguised with a pen-name and a strange typewriter have won welcome and success where the old name and the old typewriter would have insured rejection. Note this from one who has been twenty-five years at the game:

"In the near-humorous line I may mention the fact that I once tried to get the editor of a certain paper to let me furnish him a serial, but he didn't think I could write it. Soon afterward a friend who had been contributing serials to that particular paper was asked by the editor to furnish a serial. As it chanced, the writer happened to be engaged in other work. So-he came to me and wanted to know if I could not write the desired serial. When I informed him that the editor had turned my offer down, he then suggested that I write the serial and let him send it in under his own name. It was a chance to try the sagacity of that particular editor. I salved my conscience, wrote the serial, and my typewritten copy was submitted to the editor under the name of my friend. The serial was accepted, with medals thrown all over it—my literary friend being informed that it was just the thing the editor wanted, and that he had hard work to get authors who could suit his view as to what was available for his particular publication. My friend got the honor, if there was any, of seeing the serial run under his name; and I got the money for doing the work."

If an author ever suffers an editor's contempt, what must the editor suffer on being caught red-handed in such a way as this? It is the worm's prerogative to turn whenever it finds the opportunity.

Illustrating this point, and several other points with which this chapter is concerned, the following letter from another writer, who has been turning out successful manuscripts for upward of twenty years, is reproduced:

"Dear Bro. Edwards:
You certainly DO put a poser to me. At the present time I have difficulty in seeing anything that has happened to me in the twenty-odd years of my following the literary game in anything but a tragic light. I believe my success, such as it was, was tragic. At least, it has rivetted my reputation to a certain class of literature—heaven save the mark!—and makes it almost impossible for me to sell anything of a bettter quality. I might tell you of plenty of cruel things that have been done to me by publishers and editors when they knew or suspected that I was hard up; and plenty of silly things done to me by the same folk when they thought I didn't particularly NEED their money. But funny things——?

THE FICTION FACTORY

It's the point of view makes the thing funny. The child pulling the wings off a fly to see the insect crawl over the window pane is amused; but I don't suppose the fly sees the humor of the situation. I could tell you tales of submitting the same manuscript three times to an editor whom we both know well, having it shot through with criticism the first two times and then having it accepted and paid for at extra rates within two years of the first submission, and without even a word of the title changed! Is THAT the kind of an incident you want?

One of the funniest things that ever happened to me was that an editor of a popular magazine used to say that my stuff resembled Dickens, and when I wrote half-dime novels the readers used to write in and say the same. The quality of mind possessed by the scholarly editor and the street boys who read 'Bowery Billy' must be somewhat the same—eh?

There was once a magazine that bore as its title the name of a publisher as famous as any American ever saw, and the editor bought a story of me at the rate of half a cent a word, and owed me two years for it. Finally, one time when I was very hard up I went to the office and hung around until I could see the 'boss' and put it up to him to pay me. He did. He knocked off 33 1-3 per cent for 'cash.' Pretty good, eh?

I tell you, Edwards, there's nothing funny in the game that I can see—not for the so-called literary worker. The gods may laugh when they see a man with that brand of insanity on him that actually forces him to write. But I doubt if the writer laughs—not even if he writes a 'best seller.' For success entails turning out other successes, and that is hard work. Excuse me! I am going back to the farm. I will write only when I have to, and only as long as my farm will not support me. I've got hold of a pretty good place cheap, down here with the outlook of making a good living on it in time. No more the Great White Way, with the Dirty Black Alley behind it, in mine! I am not going to carry my hat in my hand around to editors' offices and take up collections for long. Besides, most of the editors blooming now are just out of college and are not dry behind the ears yet. They think that Johnny Go-bang, who edited the sporting page in the Podunk University Screamer, knows more about writing fiction than the old fellows who have been at it a couple of decades. And I reckon they are right. They are looking for 'fresh' material; some of it is pretty 'raw' as well as fresh. I fooled an editor the other day by sending a manuscript on strange paper. written on a new typewriter, and with an assumed name attached. Sold the story and got a long letter of encouragement from the editor.

Great game—encouraging 'new' writers! About on a par with
the scheme some rum sellers have of washing their sidewalks
with the dregs of beer kegs. The spider and fly game. Now,
if I told that editor what an ass he had made of himself, would
he ever buy another manuscript of me again? I fear not!

Perhaps I am pessimistic, Brother Edwards. There's no real
fun in the writing game—not for the writer, at least. Not
when he is forty years old and knows that already he is a 'has-
been.' Good luck to you. Hope your book is a success, and if
I really knew just what you wanted I'd try to whip something
into shape for you. For you very well know that, if other fiction writers give you incidents for your book, they'll mostly be
fiction! That is the devil of it. If a fiction writer cuts a
sliver off his thumb while paring the corned beef for dinner,
he will make out of the story a gory combat between his hero
and a horde of enemies, and give details of the carnage fit to
make his own soul shudder.

I hope to meet up with you again some time. But pretty
soon when I go to New York I'll wear my chin-whiskers long
and carry a carpet-bag; and you bet I'll fight shy of editors'
offices."

Another example of injustice to writers which, however, happened to turn out well for the writer:

"I offered a short serial to a certain newspaper syndicate.
Soon I received a lettter saying they could pay me $200 for the
serial rights. Before my letter accepting the offer reached
them, I had another letter from the syndicate withdrawing the
offer. The editor stated pathetically that the proprietor had returned and had asked him to withdraw it. I then sent the serial to a Chicago newspaper, which paid me $200 for serial rights
—BUT NEVER PUBLISHED THE STORY. Finally I re-
wrote the story, had it published as a book by a leading Eastern publishing house, and it sold well."

Here, again, is injustice of another kind:

"Once a certain Eastern magazine authorized me to go to
Santa Fe, New Mexico, and write a description of a Pueblo
dance and of Pueblo life, and send the manuscript on with
photographs for illustration. I did the work. And I was re-
warded by the generous editor with a check for $20! You can
imagine how profitable that particular stunt was, for I took
a week's time and paid my own expenses. But not out of that
twenty. There wasn't enough of it to go 'round."

XXIV.

WHAT SHALL
WE DO
WITH IT?

Edwards wrote only one serial story during 1910, and turned his hand to that merely to bring up the financial returns and leave a safe margin for expenses. Nickel novels, a few short stories, a novelette for *The Blue Book* and the lengthening of two stories for paper-book publication comprised the year's work. He "soldiered" a little, but when a writer "soldiers" he is not necessarily idle. Edwards' thoughts were busy, and the burden of his reflections was this: Heaven had endowed him with a small gift of plot and counter-plot, and a little art for getting it into commercial form; but were his meager talents producing for him all that they should? Was the purely commercial aim, although held to with a strong sense of moral responsibility, the correct aim? After a score of years of hard work did he find himself progressing in any but a financial direction? Forgetting the past and facing the future with eyes fixed at a higher angle, how was he to proceed with his "little gift of words?" What should he do with it?

In the bright summer afternoons Edwards would walk out of his Fiction Factory and make a survey of it from various points. He was always so close to his work that he lost the true perspective. He was familiar with the minutiae, the thousand and one little details that went to make up the whole, but how did it look in the "all-together," stripped of sentiment and beheld in its three dimensions?

Paradoxically, the work appeared too commercial in some of its aspects, and not commercial enough in others. The sordid values were due to the demand which came to Edwards constantly and unsolicited, and which it was his unvarying policy always to meet. "All's fish that comes to the writer's net" was a saying of Edwards' that had cozzened his judgment. He was giving his best to work whose very nature kept him to a dead level of mediocrity. And within the last few years he had become unpleasantly aware that at least one editor believed him incapable of better things. This was largely Edwards' fault. Orders for material along the same old lines poured in upon him and he hesitated to break away from them and try out his literary wings.

Years before he had faced a similar question. The same principal of breaking away from something that was reasonably sure and regular for something else not so sure but which glowed with brighter possibilities, was involved. Vaguely he felt the call. He was forty-four, and had left behind him twenty-odd years of hard and conscientious effort. As he was getting on in years so should he be getting on with some of his dreams, before the light failed and the Fiction Factory grew dark and all dreaming and doing were at an end.

One evening in Christmas week, 1910, he mentioned his aspirations to a noted editor with whom he happened to be at dinner. The book that was to bring fame and fortune, the book Edwards had always been going to write but had never been able to find the time, was under discussion. "Write it," advised the noted one, "but not under your own name."

Edwards fell silent. What was there in the work he had done which made it impossible to put "John Milton Edwards" on the title page of his most ambitious effort? Were the nickel novels and the popular paperbacks to rise in judgment against him? He could not think so then, and he does not think so now.

"Why don't you write up your experiences as an author?" inquired the editor a few moments later. "You want to be helpful, eh? Well, there's your chance. Writers would not be the only ones to welcome such a book, and if you did it fairly well it ought to make a hit."

This suggestion Edwards adopted. Having the courage of convictions directly opposed to the noted editor's, the other one he will not accept.

The reflections of 1910 began to bear fruit in 1911. With the beginning of the present year Edwards gave up the five-cent fiction, not because—as already stated in a previous chapter—he considered it debasing to his "art," but because he needed time for the working out of a few of his dreams.

Presently, as though to confirm him in his determination, two publishing houses of high standing requested novels to be issued with their imprint. He accepted both commissions, and at this writing the work is well advanced. If he fails of material success in either or both these undertakings, by the standards elsewhere quoted and in which he thoroughly believes, the higher success that cannot be separated from faithful effort will yet be his. And it will suffice.

Even in 1910 Edwards had been swayed by his growing convictions. Almost unconsciously he had begun shaping his work along the line of higher achievement. During 1911 he has been hewing to the same line, but more consistently.

Edwards has demonstrated his ability to write moving picture scenarios that will sell. But is the game worth the candle? Is it pleasant for an author to see his cherished Western idea worked out with painted white men for Indians and painted buttes for a background? Of course, there are photoplays enacted on the Southwestern deserts, with real cowboys and red men for "supers," but somewhere in most of these performances a false note is struck. One who knows the West has little trouble in detecting it.

This, however, is a matter of sentiment, alone. The nebulous ideas most scenario editors seem to have as to rates of payment, and the usually long delay in passing upon a "script," are important details of quite another sort. And, furthermore, it is unjust to throw a creditable production upon the screen without placing the author's name under the title. Of right, this advertising belongs to the author and should not be denied him.

In 1910 a moving picture concern secured a concession for taking pictures with Buffalo Bill's Wild West and Pawnee Bill's Far East Show, and Edwards was hired to furnish scenarios at $35 each. He furnished a good many, and of one of them Major Lillie (Pawnee Bill) wrote from Butte, Montana, on Sep. 2;
"Friend Edwards:

I saw one of the films run off at a picture house a few days ago and I think they are the greatest Western scenes that I have ever witnesed—that is, they are the truest to life. I had a letter from Mr. C—— yesterday, and he thinks they are fine.
Your friend,
"G. W. Lillie."

For a time Edwards thought his faith in the moving picture makers was about to be justified. But he was mistaken. He received a check for just $25, which probably escaped from the film men in an unguarded moment, and no further check, letter or word has since come from the company. The proprietors of the Show had nothing to do with the picture people, and regretted, though they could not help the loss Edwards had suffered.

When the moving picture writers are assured of better prices for their scenarios, of having them passed upon more promptly and of getting their names on the films with their pictures, the business will have been shaken down to a more commendable basis. Possibly the film manufacturers borrow their ideas of equitable treatment for the writer from some of the publishing houses.

The "hack" writer, in many editorial offices, is looked down upon with something like contempt by the august personage who condescends to buy his "stuff" and to pay him good money for it. Perhaps the "hack" is at fault and has placed himself in an unfavorable light. Writers are many and competition is keen. Among these humble ones there are those who have suffered rebuff after rebuff until the spirit is broken and pride is killed, and they go cringing to an editor and supplicate him for an assignment. Or they write him: "For God's sake do not turn down this story! It is the bread-line for me, if you do."

Did you ever walk through the ante-room of a big publishing house on the day checks are signed and given out? Men with pinched faces and ragged clothes sit in the mahogany chairs. They have missed the high mark in their calling. They had high ambitions once—but ambitions are always high when hope is young. They are writing now, not because they love their work but because it is the only work they know, and they must keep at it or starve (perhaps *and* starve).

A taxicab flings madly up to the door in front, and a stylishly clad gentleman floats in at the hall door and across the ante-room to the girl at the desk. They exchange pleasant greetings and the girl punches a button that communicates with the private office of the powers that be.

"Mr. Oswald Hamilton Brezee to see Mr. Skinner."

Delighted mumblings by Mr. Skinner come faintly to the ears of the lowly ones. The girl turns away from the 'phone.

"Go right in, Mr. Brezee," she says. "Mr. Skinner will see you at once."

Mr. Brezee's "stuff" has caught on. Dozens of magazines are clamoring for it. Mr. Brezee vanishes and presently reappears, tucking away his check with the careless manner of one to whom checks are more or less of a bore. He passes into the hall, and in a moment the "taxi" is heard bearing him away.

The lowly ones twist in their chairs and bitterness floods their hearts. Like the author of "Childe Harold," Brezee awoke one morning to find himself famous. These others, with the dingy Windsor ties and the long hair and pinched faces never awake to anything but a doubt as to where the morning meal is to come from.

After hours of waiting in the ante-room, checks are finally produced and passed around to the lowly ones and they fade away into the haunts that know them best. Next pay-day they will be back again, if they are alive and have been given anything to do in the meantime.

Is *this* game worth the candle? What shall these men do with their "little gift" but keep it grinding, merciless though the grind may be? They cannot all be Oswald Hamilton Brezees.

Before a young man throws himself into the ranks of this vast army of writers, let him ponder the situation well. If, under the iron heel of adversity, he is sure he can still love his work for the work's sake and be true to himself, there is one chance in ten that he will make a fair living, and one chance in a hundred that he may become one of the generals.

The Factory returns for 1910 and for part of 1911 are given below. Edwards believes that, in its last analysis, 1911 will offer figures close to the ten-thousand dollar mark—but it is a guess hedged around with many contingencies.

1910:

54 nickel novels @ $60 each,	$3240.00
Short story for Munsey's,	75.00
Short story for The Blue Book,	40.00
Novelette for The Blue Book	200.00
Moving picture, Essanay Co,	25.00
Short story for Gunter's	40.00
Short story for Columbian,	15.00
Paper-book rights,	200.00
Serial story for Scrap Book,	400.00
Moving picture,	25.00
Total	$4260.00

Part of 1911:

5 paper-book rights,	$ 500.00
Serial for All-Story,	400.00
Novelette for Adventure,	250.00
Serial for The Argosy,	250.00

THE FICTION FACTORY

Novelette for The Blue Book, ... 200.00
Short stories for The Blue Book, ... 150.00
Short story for Harper's Weekly, ... 75.00
Serial for "Top-Notch," 150.00

   Total, ...$1975.00

George Ade asked an actress, who was one of the original cast of "The County Chairman," to whom he had just been introduced, "Which would you rather be—a literary man or a burglar?" It is related that the actress, who was probably as excited as Ade, answered, "What's the difference?" And this is supposed to be a humorous anecdote!

The man who tells stories, sometimes fiction and sometmes stories, about the Harper publications, evolves the following realistic story about "The Masquerader," originally published in *The Bazaar*. Well, it seems that one morning, the editor sat her down and found the following letter, which is truly pathetic and possibly pathetically true: "You may, and I hope you have, some little remembrance of my name. But this will be the very oddest letter you have ever received I am reading that most clever and wonderfully well-written novel, "The Masquerader." I have very serious heart trouble and may live years and may die any minute. I should deeply regret going without knowing the general end of that story. May I know it? Will be as close as the grave itself if I may. I really feel that I may not live to know the unravelling of that net. If I may know for reason good and sufficient to yourself and by no means necessary to explain, may I please have the numbers as they come to you, and in advance of general delivery?" The editor sent on the balance of the story, but it was never revealed whether it made the person well again or not. Edwards imagines that the whirl of action in books would not be good for the heart—or, for the matter of that, the soul.

XXV.

EXTRACTS
GRAVE AND GAY,
WISE AND OTHERWISE

Cigars on the Editor:

"The berth check came to me this morning. I suppose the cigars are on me. At the same time, there is another kind of check which you get when you buy your Pullman accomodation at the Pullman office in the station. It was that which I had in mind. I suppose the one you enclosed is the conductor's check. I don't believe I ever saw one before."

How "Bob" Davis hands you a Lemon

"The first six or seven chapters of 'Hammerton's Vase' are very lively and readable—after which it falls off the shelf and is badly shattered. Everybody in the yarn is pretty much of a sucker, and the situations are more or less of a class. I think, John, that there is too much talk in this story. Your last thirty pages are nothing but.

What struck me most was the ease with which you might have wound the story up in any one of several places without in anyway injuring it. That is not like the old John Milton of yore. You used to pile surprise upon surprise, and tie knot after knot in your complications. But you didn't do it in 'Hammerton's Vase'—for which reason I shed tears and return the manuscript by express."

How Mr. White does it:

"I am very sorry to be obliged to make an adverse report on 'The Gods of Tlaloc.' For one thing the story is too wildly improbable, for another the hero is too stupid, and worse than all the interest is of too scrappy a nature—not cumulative. You have done too good work for The Argosy in the past for me to content myself with this....When I return Aug. 9, I shall hope to find a corking fine story from your pen awaiting my perusal. I am sure you know how to turn out such a yarn."

A tip regarding "Dual-identity":

"The story opens well, and that is the best I can say for it. I put up the scheme to Mr. Davis and he expressed a strong disinclination for any kind of a dual-identity story."—Matthew White, Jr.

How Mr. Davis takes over the Right Stuff:

"We are taking the sea story. Will report on the other stuff you have here in a day or two. In the meantime, remember that you owe me an 80,000-word story and that you are getting the maximum rate and handing me the minimum amount of words. You raised the tariff and I stood for it and it is up to you to make good some of your threats to play ball according to Hoyle. It is your turn to get in the box and bat 'em over the club-house. And remember, I am always on the bleachers, waiting to cheer at the right time."

How Mr. White lands on it:

" 'Helping Columbus' pleases me very much, and on our principle of paying for quality I am sending you for it our check for $350."

During the earlier years of his writing Edwards made use of an automatic word-counter which he attached to his Caligraph—the machine he was using at that time. He discovered that if a story called for 30,000 words, and he allowed the counter to register that number, the copy would over-run about 5,000 words. At a much later period he discovered by actual comparisons of typewritten with printed matter just the number of words each page of manuscript would average in the composing-room. From his publishers, however, he once received the following instructions:

"To enable you to calculate the number of words to write each week, we make the following suggestions: Type off a LONG paragraph from a page of one of the weeklies that has been set solid, so that the number of words in each line will correspond with the same line in print.

When you have finished the paragraph you can get the average length of the typed line as written on your machine, and by setting your bell guard at this average length you will be able to fairly approximate, line for line, manuscript and printed story.

A complete story should contain 3,000 lines. Calculating in this way, you will be able to turn in each week a story of about the right length. Our experience shows us that the calculated length of a story based on a roughly estimated number of words usually falls short of our requirements, and although to proceed in the manner suggested above may involve a little extra work—not above half an hour at the outside and on one occasion only—by it alone are we convinced that you will strike the right number of words for each issue."

"Along the Highway of Explanations":

"I cannot see 'The Yellow Streak' quite clear enough. You whoop it up pretty well for about three-quarters of the story, and then it begins to go to pieces along the highway of explanations."—Mr. Davis.

Concerning the "Rights" of a Story:

"Unless it is otherwise stipulated, WE BUY ALL MANUS-CRIPTS WITH FULL COPYRIGHT."—F. A. Munsey Co.

And again:

"The signing of the receipt places all rights in the hands of the Frank A. Munsey Company, but they will be glad to permit you to make a stage version of your story, only stipulating that in case you succeed in getting it produced, they should receive a reasonable share of the royalties.

The Last Word on the Subject:

"Mr. White has turned over to me your letter of October 12, as I usually answer letters relating to questions of copyright. I think, under the circumstances, if you want to dramatize the story we ought to permit you to do so without payment to us. The only condition we would make would be that if you get the play produced, you should print a line on the program saying,—'Dramatized from a story published in *The Argosy*,' or words to that effect."—Mr. Titherington, of *Munsey's*.

Paragraphing, Politics and Puns:

"Your paragraphs are pretty good, so far. But SHUN POLITICS AND RELIGION in any form, direct or indirect, as you would shun the devil. And please don't pun—it is so cheap."—Mr. A. A. Mosley, of *The Detroit Free Press*.

Climaxes, Snap and Spontaneity:

"We don't like to let this go back to you, and only do so in the hope that you can let us have it again. The sketch is capitally considered, the character is excellent, the way in which it is written admirable, the whole story is very funny, and yet somehow it does not quite come off. The climax—the denouement—seems somewhat labored and lacks snaps and spontaneity. Can't you devise some other termination—something with more 'go?' This is so good we want it to be better."—Editor *Puck*.

Novelty and Exhilarating Effect:

"We have no special subject to suggest for a serial, but would cheerfully read any you think desirable for our needs. The better plan always is to submit the first two installments of about four columns each. Novelty and exhilarating effect are desirable."—Editor *Saturday Night.*

Saddling and Bridling Pegasus:

"We are very much in need of a short Xmas poem—from 16 to 20 lines—to be used at once. Knowing your ability and willingness to accomodate at short notice, I write you to ask if you can get one to us by Saturday of this week, or Monday at latest. I know it is a very short time in which to saddle and bridle Pegasus, but I am sure you can do it with celerity if any one can."—Editor *The Ladies' World.*

Carrying the Thing too Far:

"We regret that we cannot make use of 'The Brand of Cain,' after your prompt response to our call, but the title and story are JUST A LITTLE BIT too sensational for our paper. and we think it best to return it to you. It is a good story, and well written, but we get SO MUCH condemnation from our subscribers, often for a trifle, that we are obliged to be very careful. Only a week or two ago we were severely censured because a recipe in Household Dep't called for a tablespoonful of wine in a pudding sauce, and the influence of the writer against the paper promised if the offense were repeated."—From the editor of a woman's journal.

And, finally, this from Mr. Davis:

"We are of the non-complaining species, ourself, and aim only to please the mob. Rush the sea story. If it isn't right, I'll rush it back, by express....Believe, sir, that I am personally disposed to regard you as a better white man than the average white man because you a larger white man, and, damnitsir, I wish you good luck."

XXII.

PATRONS AND
PROFITS FOR
TWENTY-TWO YEARS

On the 20th of this month (September, 1911) it will be just twenty-two years since Edwards received payment for his first story. On Sept. 20, 1889,, *The Detroit Free Press* sent him a check for $8. On that $8 the Fiction Factory was started.

Who have been the patrons of the Factory for these twenty-two years, and what have been the returns?

A vast amount of work has been necessary in order to formulate exact answers to these questions. Papers and other memoranda bearing upon the subject were widely scattered. During Edwards' travels about the country many letters and records were lost. The list that follows, therefore, is incomplete, but exact as far as it goes. More work was realized upon, by several thousands of dollars, than is here shown. For every item in the record Edwards has a letter, or a printed slip that accompanied the check, as his authority. The errors are merely those of omission.

Titles of the material sold will not be given, but following the name of the publication that purchased the material will be found the year in which it was either published or paid for.

Adventure, The Ridgway Company, Spring & Mac-
   dougal Streets, New York City, 1911—1 novel-
   ette. ....$ 250.
All-Story Magazine, The F. A. Munsey Co., 175
   Fifth Ave., New York City, 1904—1 serial......   225.
   1905—2 short stories, 1 serial.. ....   255.
   1906—2 serials. ....   950.
   1908—3 serials. ....   1,000.
American Press Association, 45 & 47 Park Place,
New York City, 1905—2 short stories..............   30.
The Argosy, F. A. Munsey Co., 175 Fifth Ave., New
   York City, 1900—1 serial. ....   250.
   1901—1 serial. ....   200.
   1902—1 serial. ....   250.
   1903—1 novelette, 4 serials. ....   1,050.
   1904—1 short story, 1 novelette, 4 serials..   975.
   1905—3 serials, 1 novelette. ....   925.
   1906—2 serials. ....   600.
   1911—1 serial. ....   250.
Boston Globe, Boston, Mass., 1897—1 short story...   4.
Boyce's Monthly, Chicago, Ills., 1901—1 short story.   10.
Banner Weekly, The, Beadle & Adams, New York
   City, 1889—1 short story........................   2.
Blue Book, The, Chicago, Ills., 1907—1 novelette....   220.
   1908—2 novelettes. ....   400.
   1910—1 short story, 1 novelette. ....   240.
   1911—1 novelette, 3 short stories. ....   350.
Chips, Frank Tousey's Publishing House, New York
   City, 1901—1 short story. ....   4.
Chatter, 12 Beekman St., New York, 1890—1 short
   story. ....   5.
   —1 short story. ....   5.
Chicago Inter-Ocean, Chicago, Ills., 1898—1 article,
   space rates. 2.50
Chicago Record, Chicago, Ills., 1897—1 short story..   5.
   1898—1 short story. ....   7.
   —1 short story. ....   4.
   1901—- short story. ....   6.
Chicago Daily News, Chicago, Ills.,1898—1 short
   story. ....   3.
   1899—1 short story. 3.50
   1899—4 short stories. 14.50
   1901—1 short story. ....   5.
Chicago Blade, Chicago, Ills., 1891—2 articles, space
   rates, 1 short story. ....   10.
Chicago Ledger, Chicago, Ills., 1891—3 serials. ......   120.
   1892—2 serials. ....   55.
   1896—1 serial. ....   50.
   1904—1 serial. ....   75.
   1905—2 serials. ....   80.
   1906—2 serials. ....   100.
   1907—1 serial. ....   75.
Columbian Magazine, New York City, 1910—1 short
   story. ....   15.
Demorest's Monthly, New York City, 1899—1 article.   5.
Dillingham Co., G. W., New York City, 1903—royal
   ties. $6.60
   1906—royalties. 10.20
   1908—royalties. 1.50

```
            1909—Cloth book rights. ...................  100.
Detroit Free Press, The, Detroit, Michigan..........
            1889—1 short  story. ......................    8.
               —1 short  story. ......................    7.
            1890—2 serials. ...........................  203.
            1889—2 short stories. .....................   23.
            1891—1 short story, space rates. ..........   95.
            1892—6 short stories. .....................   48.50
            1893—1 short  story. ......................   10.
            1894—1 space  rate. .......................   20.
            1895—1 space  rate. .......................   22.
            1896—1 short  story. ......................    1.50
            1899—2 short stories. .....................    7.
            1900—1 short  story. ......................    3.
Essanay Film Manufacturing Company, Chicago,
    Illinois. ......................................
            1910—  M. P. scenario. ...................   25.
Figaro, 170 Madison St., Chicago, ..................
            1890—1 space  rate. .......................   30.
            1891—1 space  rate. .......................   90.
            1892—1 space  rate. .......................   10.
Frank Leslie's Popular Monthly, 110 Fifth Ave., New
    York City ....................................
            1891—1 short  story. ......................    8.
Gunter's Magazine, Street & Smith, New York City..
            1910—1 short  story. ......................   40.
Harper's Weekly, New York City. ...................
            1911—1 short  story. ......................   75.
Illustrated American, 1123 Broadway, New York City
            1896—2 verses. ...........................   10.
Kellogg Newspaper Co., The A. N., 71-73 W. Adams
    St,, Chicago, ................................
            1903—1 serial. ...........................  115.
Life, New York City .............................
            1897—1 short  story. ......................    3.
Ledger Monthly, Ledger Building, N. Y. ............
            1899—1 short  story. ......................   10.
Lubin Mfg. Co., Philadelphia, Pa. ................
            1910—M. P. senario...................   30.
Ladies' World, The, New York City...............
            1890—2 short stories. .....................    8.
            1891—1 verse. ............................    2.
               —1 verse. ............................    2.
            1892—2 verses. ...........................    4.
            1894—1 verse. ............................    2.
            1898—1 short  story. ......................    2.
McClure's Newspaper Syndicate, The, 116 Nassau St.,
    New York City, ...............................
            1901—2 short stories, 2 serials. ..........  295.
               —1 serial. ............................  200.
McC's Monthly, Detroit, Michigan, .................
            1898—2 short stories. .....................   10.
Munsey's Magazine, New York City, ...............
            1896—1 short  story. ......................   10.
            1904—1 short  story. ......................   40.
            1910—1 short  story. ......................   75.
New York World, New York City, .................
            1894—1 short  story. ......................    5.64
```

$10,32914

Brought forward..............................$10,329.14

1897—2 short stories.	15.02
1898—1 short story.	4.68
1899—1 short story.	5.50
Overland Monthly, 508 Montgomery St., San Francisco, 1897—1 short story	10.
Ocean, F. A. Munsey Co., New York City, 1907—1 serial.	450.
People's Magazine, The, Street & Smith, New York City,	
1906—1 serial.	200.
1907—1 serial.	250.
1908—2 serials.	600.
Popular Magazine, The, Street & Smith, New York City,	
1904—2 novelettes.	265.
1909—1 serial.	200.
Puck, Keppler & Schwartzmann, Puck Building, New York City,1891—2 short stories.	20.
1892—1 short story.	5.
1893—2 short stories, 1 verse.	14.
1896—1 short story.	6.
1897—2 short stories, 1 verse.	22.
1899—2 short stories.	17.
Railroad Man's Magazine, F. A. Munsey Co., New York, 1906—2 serials.	700.
1907—1 serial.	500.
1908—2 serials.	650.
1909—2 short stories.	70.
Red Book, Chicago, Ills., 1906—1 short story.	75.
1909—1 short story.	40.
Scrap Book, F. A. Munsey Co., N. Y. C,, 1905—1 serial.	200.
1908—1 serial.	300.
1910—1 serial.	400.
1911—1 serial.	400.
Saturday Times, The, Chicago, Ills., 1907—1 serial.	60.
Southern Tobacco Journal, Winston, N. C., 1897—1 verse.	2.
Short Stories, Current Literature Pub. Co., New York City, 1891—1 short story,	5.
1898—2 short stories.	10.
1900—2 short stories.	30.
San Francisco Chronicle, San Fran., 1896—1 short story.	6.
Saturday Night, James Elverson Pub. Philadelphia, Pa., 1890—1 serial.	75.
1891—1 serial, 8 short stories.	166.
1892—5 short stories.	10.
1893—1 serial, 5 short stories.	160.
Truth, 203 Broadway, New York City, 1893—1 short story.	3.50
1897—7 short stories.	57.
Top-Notch Magazine, Street & Smith, New York City, 1911—1 serial.	150.
Translation Rights, 1908	40.
Vitagraph Company of America, The, Brooklyn, N. Y., 1909—M. P.	10.
Wayside Tales, Detroit Monthly Publishing Co., Detroit, Mich.. 1901—3 short stories.	23.

```
1902—2 short stories. .....................        35.
1903—1 short story. ........................        15.
White Elephant, Frank Tousey's Pub. House, New
    York City, 1897—2 short stories..............     30.
Western World, Chicago, Ills., 1900—2 serials, 7
    short stories,1 space rates. ...................  308.80
Woman's Home Companion, New York, 1905—1
    serial, space rate. ...........................  205.
Yankee Blade, Boston, Mass., 1890—2 short stories.   20.
    1891—3 short stories, 2 verses. .............     13.
    1893—1 short story. ........................       6.50
         —1 short story. ........................      4.
Powers Company, New York City, 1910—M. P......       25.
Street & Smith, New York City, 1909—34 issues
    "Motor Boys" ................................   2,550.
    1908— 7 paper-book rights. .................      700.
    1909—21 paper-book rights. .................    2,100.
    1910— 2 paper-book rights. .................      200.
    1911— 5 paper-book rights. .................      500.
Dodd, Mead & Co., New York City, 1904—Cloth book
    rights. .....................................     200.
Harte & Perkins, New York, Nickel Novels:........$ 23,964.44
    1893— 4 @ $ 50 each,. .....................      200.
    1894— 3 @ $ 50 each,. .....................      150.
         —31 @ $ 40 each,. .....................      960.
    1896—24 @ $ 40 each,. .....................      960.
    1897— 2 @ $ 40 each,. .....................       80.
    1898—16 @ $ 40 each,. .....................      640.
    1899—35 @ $ 40 each,. .....................    1,400.
    1900—51 @ $ 40 each,. .....................    2,040.
    Completing story. ..........................       20.
    1901—10 @ $ 30 each,. .....................      300.
         — 8 @ $ 50 each,. .....................      400.
         —16 @ $ 40 each,. .....................      640.
    1902—31 @ $ 40 each,. .....................    1,240.
    1903—44 @ $ 40 each,. .....................    1,760.
    1904—26 @ $ 40 each,. .....................    1,040.
         — 4 @ $ 50 each,. .....................      200.
    1905—10 @ $ 50 each,. .....................      500.
    1906—18 @ $ 50 each,. .....................      900.
    1907—33 @ $ 50 each,. .....................    1,650.
    1908—45 @ $ 50 each,. .....................    2,250.
    1909— 9 @ $ 60 each,. .....................      540.
    1910—54 @ $ 60 each,. .....................    3,240.
    Ten-Cent Novels:
    1893—13 @ $100 each,. .....................    1,300.
    1894—10 @ $100 each,. .....................    1,000.
    1895— 2 @ $ 40 eaech,. .....................     100.
    Serials for "Guest;"
    1894— 2 @ $300 each,. .....................      600.
         — 2 @ $500 & $400 ...................      900.
    1897— 1. ...................................     300.
    1895— 2 @ $300 & $200. ...................      500.
    1898— 2 @ $300. ...........................     600.
    1899— 1. ...................................     300.
    1906— 1. ...................................     250.
    1907— 1. ...................................     300.
                                            ─────────────
                                            $ 64,363.44
```

Brought forward............... $64,363.44
  Juvenile Serials:
  1893— 2 @ $100 & $75. .... 175.
  1894— 1. .... 175.
  1894— 1. .... 100.
  1901— 4 @ $100 each,. .... 400.
  1902— 4 @ $100 each,. .... 400.
  Miscellaneous:
  1897— 4 magazine sketches. .... 40.
   — 1 magazine sketches. 6.16
  1900—10 trade-paper sketches. .... 100.
  1901— 9 trade-paper sketches. .... 90.
  1902— 1 trade-paper sketch. .... 10.

 Total ....$ 65,859.60

The finest music in the room is that which streams out to the ear of the spirit in many an exquisite strain from the hanging shelf of books on the opposite wall. Every volume there is an instrument which some melodist of the mind created and set vibrating with music, as a flower shakes out its perfume or a star shakes out its light. Only listen, and they soothe all care, as though the silken-soft leaves of poppies had been made vocal and poured into the ear.— *James Lane Allen.*

When William Dean Howells occupied an editorial chair in Harper's office, a young man of humble and rough exterior one day submitted personally to him a poem. Mr. Howells asked:

"Did you write this poem yourself?"

"Yes, sir. Do you like it?" the youth asked.

"I think it is magnificent," said Mr. Howells. "Did you compose it unaided?"

"I certainly did," said the young man firmly. "I wrote every line of it out of my head."

Mr. Howells rose and said:

"Then, Lord Byron, I am very glad to meet you. I was under the impression that you died a good many years ago."

www.ingramcontent.com/pod-product-compliance
Lightning Source LLC
Chambersburg PA
CBHW031300090426
42742CB00007B/538